HUMANS NEED NOT APPLY

NEW HAVEN AND LONDON

Yale UNIVERSITY PRESS

# HUMANS NEED NOT APPLY

A Guide to Wealth and Work in
the Age of Artificial Intelligence

JERRY KAPLAN

Published with assistance from the foundation established in memory of Calvin Chapin of the Class of 1788, Yale College.

Yale University Press books may be purchased in quantity for educational, business, or promotional use. For information, please e-mail sales.press@yale.edu (U.S. office) or sales@yaleup.co.uk (U.K. office).

Designed by Sonia Shannon.

Set in The Sans type by Integrated Publishing Solutions, Grand Rapids, Michigan.

Printed in the United States of America.

Library of Congress Control Number: 2015930743

ISBN 978-0-300-21355-3 (cloth : alk. paper)

ISBN 978-0-300-22357-6 (pbk.)

A catalogue record for this book is available from the British Library.

10 9 8 7 6 5 4 3 2 1

*For Camryn Paige Kaplan*

Turn your dreams into words and make them true.

# Contents

I'm an optimist. Not by nature, but by U.S. government design.

After Russia humiliated the United States with the 1957 launch of Sputnik, the first space satellite, the government decided that science education should be a national priority. The cold war was in full swing, and Senator John F. Kennedy made closing the "missile gap" a centerpiece of his presidential campaign. Ceding leadership in this critical emerging arena was unthinkable.

Young boys like me (but tragically, not many girls) were fed a steady diet of utopian imagery extolling technological innovation as the path to eternal peace and prosperity, not to mention a way to beat them clever Russkies. Dog-eared copies of *Amazing Stories* and *Fantastic Adventures* illustrated how spaceships and ray guns would help you save the world and get the girl.

When I moved to New York at the age of ten, the city seemed the Land of Oz to me, and the 1964 World's Fair was the Emerald City. For less than the two dimes tucked into my Buster Brown penny loafers, I could catch the IRT at Grand Central Station to visit sparkling visions of the future like the Unisphere, the Monorail, and General Electric's Progressland, where Disney's animatronic robots would herald "a great big beautiful tomorrow" in cheerful harmony.

The world of science fiction seemed to grow up right alongside me. As I struggled with calculus and solid geometry, *Star Trek* offered solace and encouragement—surely Captain Kirk had aced his SATs. But *2001: A Space Odyssey* took things to a new level with a mystical glimpse of the destiny of humankind. Mesmerized by the infinite red halo of the Hal 9000, I knew what I had to do.

Ten years later, after earning a B.A. in history and philosophy of science at the University of Chicago and a Ph.D. in computer science at the University of Pennsylvania, I accepted a research position in the Stanford Artificial Intelligence Lab.

I thought I had died and gone to heaven. Inhabited by disheveled geniuses and quirky wizards, the dilapidated lab sat atop an isolated rise in the gentle hills west of Stanford's campus. Strange electronic music wafted through the halls at odd hours; robots occasionally moseyed aimlessly around the parking lot. Logicians debated with philosophers over whether machines could have minds. John McCarthy—founder of the lab, who coined the term *artificial intelligence,* or AI—haunted the halls stroking his pointed beard. A large clearing inside the semicircular structure seemed to await first contact with an advanced extraterrestrial civilization.

But even in paradise, the natives can grow restless. Silicon Valley made its siren call—a chance to change the world and get rich at the same time. We had been scrounging around for research funds to build our projects; now a new class of financiers—venture capitalists—came calling with their bulging bankrolls.

Several startup companies and thirty years later, I finally curbed my entrepreneurial enthusiasm and retired, only to find I wasn't quite prepared to fade quietly into my dotage. A chance encounter opened a new door; I was invited to return to the Stanford

AI Lab, but this time as a gray-haired patrician, knowledgeable in the ways of the big, bad commercial world.

To my surprise, the lab was completely different. The people were just as bright and enthusiastic, but the sense of common mission was gone. The field had fragmented into a number of subspecialties, making cross-disciplinary dialog more difficult. Most people were so focused on their next breakthrough that I felt they had lost sight of the broader picture. The original goal of the field—to discover the fundamental nature of intelligence and reproduce it in electronic form—had given way to elegant algorithms and clever demos.

In the hopes of rekindling the original spirit of the lab, I offered to teach a course on the history and philosophy of artificial intelligence. But as I dived into the subject matter, I became acutely aware of some serious issues looming on the horizon.

Having witnessed enough frames of the movie, I could see that a happy ending is anything but assured. Recent advances in the field are poised to make an astonishing impact on society, but whether we will make a graceful transition or emerge bruised and battered is uncertain.

The brilliant and dedicated people in the Stanford AI Lab—and their many colleagues in universities, research centers, and corporations around the world—are working on the twenty-first-century moral equivalent of the Manhattan Project. And, like the staff of that supersecret project to develop the atom bomb, only a few are cognizant of the breathtaking potential of their work to transform lives and livelihoods, right down to altering our concept of who we are and our proper place in the universe. It's one thing to make a cute little robot that reads names and addresses, then tootles down the hall delivering intramural mail, but quite another when incrementally more capable versions of this technology operate our farms, manage our pension funds, hire and fire workers, select which news stories we read, scan all our communications for subversive ideas, and fight our wars.

Sure, but that's science fiction. We've seen this kind of stuff in the movies for decades and nothing terrible has happened in real life. So what's the big deal? Why all the fuss now?

HUMANS NEED NOT APPLY

# Welcome to the Future

n a nutshell, after fifty years of effort and billions spent on research, we're cracking the code on artificial intelligence. It turns out that it's not the same as human intelligence, or at least it looks that way right now. But that doesn't matter. In the words of computer scientist Edsger Dijkstra, "The question of whether machines can think is about as relevant as the question of whether submarines can swim." Whether the website that finds you a date or the robot that cuts your grass will do it the same way you do doesn't matter. It will get the job done more quickly, accurately, and at a lower cost than you possibly can.

Recent advances in robotics, perception, and machine learning, propelled by accelerating improvements in computer technology, are enabling a new generation of systems that rival or exceed human capabilities. These developments are likely to usher in a new age of unprecedented prosperity and leisure, but the transition may be protracted and brutal. Without adjustments to our economic system and regulatory policies, we may be in for an extended period of social turmoil.

The warning signs are everywhere. The two great scourges of the modern developed world—persistent unemployment and increasing income inequality—plague our society even as our economy continues to grow. If these are left unchecked, we may witness the spectacle of widespread poverty against a backdrop of escalating comfort and wealth. My goal is to give you a personal tour of the breakthroughs fueling this transition and the challenges it poses for society. I will also suggest some free-market solutions that promote progress while reducing government intrusion in our lives.

The work in artificial intelligence is advancing on two fronts. New systems of the first class, many of which are already deployed, learn from experience. But unlike humans, who are limited in the scope and scale of experiences they can absorb, these systems can scrutinize mountains of instructive examples at blinding speeds. They are capable of comprehending not only the visual, auditory, and written information familiar to us but also the more exotic forms of data that stream through computers and networks. Imagine how smart you would be if you could see through thousands of eyes, hear distant sounds, and read every word as it is published. Then slow the world down to a pace where you can sample and ponder all of this at your leisure, and you'll get an idea of how these systems experience their environment.

As we amass data from an expanding array of sensors that monitor aspects of the physical world—air quality, traffic flow, ocean wave heights—as well as our own electronic footprints such as ticket sales, online searches, blog posts, and credit card transactions, these systems can glean patterns and grasp insights inaccessible to the human mind. You might reasonably describe them as exhibiting superhuman intelligence, but that's misleading—at least for the foreseeable future—because these machines aren't conscious, self-reflective, and don't exhibit any hint of independent aspirations or personal desires. In other words, they don't have minds, as we commonly understand the word. They are incredibly good at specific tasks, but we don't fully understand how they do what they do. In most cases, that's because there is literally no explanation that can be comprehended by simple creatures like us.

This area of research doesn't have a universally accepted name. Depending on the focus and approach, researchers call it machine learning, neural networks, big data, cognitive systems, or genetic algorithms, among others. I will simply refer generically to the product of their efforts as *synthetic intellects*.

Synthetic intellects are not programmed in the conventional sense. You cobble them together from a growing collection of tools and modules, establish a goal, point them to a trove of examples, and set them loose. Where they wind up is unpredictable and not under their creator's control. Synthetic intellects will soon know more about you than your mother does, be able to predict your behavior better than you can, and warn you of dangers you can't even perceive. I will describe in some detail how synthetic intellects work and why they transcend our common preconceptions of what computers can do.

The second class of new systems arises from the marriage of sensors and actuators. They can see, hear, feel, and interact with their surroundings. When they're bundled together, you can recognize these systems as "robots," but putting them into a single physical package is not essential. In fact, in most cases it's undesirable. The sensors may be sprinkled throughout an environment, on the tops of streetlights or in other people's smartphones, with their observations harvested and siloed in some distant server farm, which then uses this information to formulate a plan. The plan may be executed directly, by controlling remote devices, or indirectly, for example, by coaxing you to take some desired action. Often, the results of these actions are immediately sensed, leading to continuous revision of the plan, just as you do when you guide your hand to pick up an object.

You are part of such a system when you follow automated driving directions. The program, monitoring your location and speed (usually by GPS), directs you, often pooling your information with that of other drivers to detect traffic conditions, which it uses in turn to route you (and them) more efficiently.

Perhaps the most remarkable of these systems will appear deceptively simple, because they accomplish physical tasks that people consider routine. While they lack common sense and general intelligence, they can tirelessly perform an astonishing range of chores in chaotic, dynamic environments.

To date, automation has mostly meant special-purpose machines relegated to performing repetitive, single tasks on factory floors, where the environment is designed around them. In contrast, these new systems will be out and about, tending fields, painting houses, cleaning sidewalks, washing and folding laundry. They may be working in concert with human workers to lay pipes, harvest crops, and build houses, or they may be deployed independently in dangerous or inaccessible places to fight fires, inspect bridges, mine the seabed, and fight wars. I will refer to these embodied systems as *forged laborers*.

Of course, these two types of systems—synthetic intellects and forged laborers—can work in unison to perform physical tasks that require a high level of knowledge and skill, such as fixing cars, performing surgery, and cooking gourmet meals.

In principle, all these developments will not only free you from drudgery but make you more efficient and effective, if you're lucky enough to be able to afford them. Bespoke electronic agents may promote your personal interests, represent you in negotiations, and teach you calculus—but not all such systems will be working on your behalf.

Humans are suckers for the quick win. What Jaron Lanier presciently calls "siren servers" will custom-tailor short-term incentives to your desires, persuading you to do things that may not be in your long-term interests.[1] The irresistible lure of temporary bargains and faster delivery may obscure the gradual destruction of the lifestyle that you hold near and dear. You can order a new rice cooker online tonight and get it delivered tomorrow, but the cost doesn't include the gradual closing of retail stores near your home and the neighbors it puts out of work.

It's one thing for these systems to recommend what music you should listen to or what toothbrush you should buy. It's quite another when we permit them to take action on their own—or, to use today's buzzword, make them autonomous. Because they operate on timescales we can barely perceive, with access to volumes of data we can't comprehend, they can wreak havoc on an unimaginable scale in the blink of an eye—shutting down electrical grids, placing all airplane takeoffs on hold, canceling millions of credit cards.

You might wonder why someone would build a system that could do such things. It's simple prudence to design in safeguards that protect against rare events, such as simultaneous short circuits in two or more critical power transmission lines. These catastrophic, once-a-century events somehow seem to happen with alarming regularity. When they do, there isn't time for a so-called human in the loop to review the decision in context because the damage is done literally at the speed of light. As scary as it sounds, the launch of a Russian nuclear missile would at least afford us a few minutes to consider an appropriate course of action, but a cyber attack on a nuclear power plant could disable its control systems in an instant. So we have little choice but to trust the machines to protect us.

In the untamed wilds of cyberspace, you never know when two or more autonomous systems whose goals are in conflict may encounter each other. The scale and speed of the resultant electronic brawl can take on the characteristics of a natural disaster. This isn't hypothetical—it's already happened with horrific effects.

On May 6, 2010, the stock market inexplicably plunged 9 percent (one thousand points on the Dow Jones Industrial Average), most of the drop taking place in a matter of minutes. Over $1 trillion in asset value temporarily evaporated, money that represented the retirement savings of millions of workers, among other things. Specialists on the floors of the stock exchanges were left scratching their heads in disbelief.

It took the U.S. Securities and Exchange Commission nearly six months to figure out what had happened, and the answer is hardly comforting: Competing computer programs, buying and selling stocks on behalf of their owners, had gotten out of control. In the murky, secretive world known as high-frequency trading, these systems not only reap small profit opportunities that appear and disappear in an instant but also detect and exploit each other's trading strategies.[2]

What the creators of these electronic card sharks couldn't anticipate was the effect of their programs on each other. Designers develop and test their sophisticated models using historical data, and so cannot predict the presence and behavior of equally capable opposing forces. The seemingly random clash of these titans shook the very foundation of our financial system, which is our faith in its fairness and stability. Economists give this strange new phenomenon the unassuming name of "systemic risk," which makes it sound like something that can be fixed with a shot of regulatory penicillin and a good night's sleep.

But the root cause is much more sinister—the emergence of invisible electronic agents empowered to take actions on behalf of the narrow self-interests of their owners, without regard to the consequences for the rest of the world. Because these agents are stealthy and incorporeal, we can't perceive their presence or comprehend their capabilities. We'd be better off with robotic muggers —at least we could see them coming and run away.

The "Flash Crash" of 2010 may have caught regulators' attention, but it did nothing to slow the application of similar techniques to a wide variety of other domains. Any time you buy something, visit a website, or post a comment online, a hidden army of electronic agents, working for someone else, is watching you. Whole industries have sprung up that do nothing but sell weapons in the form of programs and data to companies brave enough to wade into these never-ending melees. Later in this book I will describe one such arena in detail: the monumental cluster fight that takes place behind the scenes for the right to show you an ad every time you load a web page.

The emergence of powerful autonomous agents raises serious ethical questions. Much of the way we allocate shared resources among people follows unstated social conventions. The town regulations near my house permit me to park in a spot for up to two hours, on the assumption that it is inconvenient for me to move my car that often. But what if my car can change spots by itself? Will my personal robot be permitted to stand in line at the movie theater on my behalf?

Autonomous cars, which are only a few years from broad deployment, raise much more serious issues. The split-second decisions these contraptions will have to make pose ethical questions that have bedeviled deep thinkers for millennia. Imagine that my car is crossing a narrow bridge and a school bus full of children suddenly enters from the other side. The bridge can't accommodate both vehicles, so to avoid destroying both it's clear that one of them will have to go over the edge. Would I buy a car that is willing to sacrifice my life to save the children? Will the aggressiveness of a self-driving car become a selling point like gas mileage? Moral quandaries like this, no longer confined to the musings of philosophers, will urgently arrive on our courthouse steps.

The emergence of synthetic intellects and forged laborers that act as our individual agents will raise a raft of practical conundrums. What should "one per customer" mean when a robot is the customer, and I own a whole fleet of them? Can my personal electronic assistant lie on my behalf? Should it be required to report me if I direct it to serve my twenty-year-old daughter wine at Thanksgiving dinner?

Society crafts laws and regulations on the assumption that people can occasionally exercise a certain amount of individual discretion. How will you feel about a dog-walking robot that fails to save your child from being mauled because it is obeying a "Keep off the grass" sign? Or an autonomous car that refuses to speed you to the hospital to save you from a heart attack? Our institutions will soon have to grapple with balancing the needs of individuals against the wider interests of society in a whole new way.

But all of this pales in comparison to the economic dangers these systems pose. A broad cross section of today's blue-collar and white-collar jobs will soon come under threat from forged laborers and synthetic intellects respectively. An astonishing range of productive activities, both physical and mental, will become vulnerable to replacement by these new devices and programs. Why should someone hire you instead of buying one of them?

We're about to discover that Karl Marx was right: the inevitable struggle between capital (whose interests are promoted by management) and labor is a losing proposition for workers. What he didn't fully appreciate is that we're all workers, even managers, doctors, and college professors. As an economist, Marx understood that industrial automation substitutes capital for your labor, even if he didn't quite have forged laborers in mind. But what he couldn't foresee is that synthetic intellects can also substitute capital for your mind. So the conflict he characterizes between poorly paid workers and highly compensated managers—people against people—cuts the wrong way. The real problem is that the wealthy will need few, if any, people to work for them at all.

As bizarre as this sounds, the future will be a struggle of assets against people, as the resources accumulated by our creations serve no constructive purpose or are put to no productive use. As I will explain, the so-called 1 percent may be the beneficiaries of these trends today, but without some careful precautions as to who—or what—may own assets, there's a real possibility that the 1 percent will shrink to the 0 percent, just as the pyramids of ancient Egypt drained the resources of an entire society to serve the personal whims of a single ruler. The economy we know today, as difficult to manage as it may be, is in danger of motoring on without us, throwing ever more of us overboard. Will the last human dismissed please turn off the lights? Actually, no need—they can turn themselves off.

But there are even greater risks. When we think of AI, we tend to picture a future full of robots as docile servants or malevolent overlords (take your pick), or giant computer brains buried in fortified bunkers. There's nothing quite like the image of a grimacing cyborg to raise your hackles. But this is just our anthropomorphic bias and countless Hollywood treatments leading us astray. The real danger comes from distributed armies of tiny forged laborers organized like swarms of insects, and disembodied synthetic intellects residing on remote servers in the cloud. It's hard to worry about threats that you can't see or perceive. Things can just seem to inexplicably get worse. The Luddites of the early Industrial Revolution could smash the looms that took their jobs, but how can you fight back against a smartphone app?

Modern policy makers are wringing their hands over the root causes of persistent unemployment and economic inequality, but certainly one underappreciated driver is accelerating technological progress. As I will demonstrate, advances in information technology are already gutting industries and jobs at a furious clip, far faster than the labor markets can possibly adapt, and there's much worse to come. They are also substituting capital for labor in completely new ways, delivering a disproportionate share of new wealth to the already rich.

The usual rejoinder to this is that the improved productivity will increase wealth, floating all our boats, and that new jobs will emerge to cater to our expanding desires and needs. True enough— in aggregate and on average. But when you dig deeper, this doesn't necessarily mean that we are better off. With labor markets, as with global warming, it's the pace that matters, not the fact. Current workers may have neither the time nor the opportunity to acquire the skills required by these new jobs. And average income doesn't matter if a small cadre of superwealthy oligarchs takes the lion's share while everyone else lives in relative poverty. Increasing wealth may float all yachts while sinking all rowboats.

In the first chapters of this book I will lay out some foundational concepts and ideas required to reframe the ongoing policy debates. I will attempt to demystify the magic under the hood by explaining why most of what you believe about computers is wrong. Unless you understand what's really happening, you can't appreciate what's likely to happen in the future.

Then I will suggest practical solutions to some of the most serious issues, such as how we can extend our legal system to regulate and hold autonomous systems responsible for their actions. But the economic consequences are by far the most serious problems we will have to address. The obvious simple solution, to redistribute the wealth from the rich to the poor, is a nonstarter in our current political environment. It also doesn't address the underlying cause of the problems; it just stirs up the pot in the hope of preventing it from coming to a boil. Instead, I will present a framework that applies free-market solutions to address the underlying structural problems we are creating.

Unemployment is going to be a serious problem—but not, surprisingly, because of a lack of jobs. Rather, the skills required to do the available jobs are likely to evolve more quickly than workers can adapt without significant changes to how we train our workforce. Our current sequential system of education and work—first you go to school, then you get a job—was fine when you could expect to do more or less the same thing for a living throughout your working life. But looking forward, it simply isn't going to work. The nature of the jobs available will shift so rapidly that you may find your skills obsolete just when you thought you were starting to get ahead. Our current system of vocational training, largely a holdover from medieval apprenticeships and indentured servitude, is in need of significant modernization.

I will propose an approach to this problem in the form of a new type of financial instrument, the "job mortgage," secured exclusively by your future labor (earned income) similar to the way your home mortgage is secured exclusively by your property. Out of work? Payments are suspended for some reasonable grace period, until you find another job.

In the proposed system, employers and schools will have incentives to collaborate in a new way. Employers will issue nonbinding letters of intent to hire you if you acquire specified skills, and they will get certain payroll tax breaks if they ultimately follow through. These letters of intent will serve the same purpose for job mortgage lenders as an appraisal serves for a home mortgage lender. Training institutions will have to craft their curricula around the specific skills required by sponsoring employers in order to meet the requirements of the loans, or else students won't enroll. You won't be committed in advance to accepting a particular position if someone else makes you a better offer, but at least you have the comfort of knowing that you are acquiring the skills valued by the marketplace. In effect, this scheme introduces a new form of feedback and liquidity into labor markets, enforced through the discipline of the free market.

But our greatest societal challenge will be to rein in growing income inequality. I will propose an objective, government-certified measure of corporate ownership, which I will call the public benefit index, or PBI, which can serve as the foundation for a variety of programs to keep society on a more even keel. By scaling corporate taxes based on how many stockholders benefit from a company's success, we can tilt the scales in favor of broad public participation in an asset-based economy. But how can the average Joe and Jane afford to buy assets? For starters, they already own more than you might expect, in the form of pension funds and Social Security—they just don't know it because an opaque system of fiduciaries manage their wealth instead of them. We need to give people more visibility and control over their nest eggs, with incentives to direct the assets toward high-PBI companies. A side benefit is social stability. The temptation to riot and loot the local department store is greatly diminished if you know you are a stockholder.

We don't need to take from the wealthy and give to the less fortunate because our economy is not standing still; it's continually expanding, and this growth is likely to quicken. So all we need to do is distribute the benefits of future growth more widely, and the problem will slowly melt away. A carefully crafted program of tax incentives, portfolio transparency, and increased individual control over asset allocation based on the PBI offers us a way to keep from capsizing in the rising tide of concentrating prosperity.

So why can't our chosen leaders better assess the situation and take corrective actions? Because you can't steer when you can't see, and you can't discuss what you can't articulate. At the moment, our public discourse lacks the concepts and exemplars to properly describe what's likely to happen as technological progress accelerates, much less to guide us to reasonable solutions.

Letting nature take its course—as we did during the Industrial Revolution of the late eighteenth and early nineteenth centuries—is a dangerous gamble. Per capita income rose dramatically, but the changes entailed untold human suffering during an extended period of economic transformation. We can ignore the coming storm and eventually everything will work out fine, but "eventually" is a long time. Without some foresight and action now, we may condemn our descendants to half a century or more of poverty and inequality, except for a lucky chosen few. Everyone likes to play the lottery—until the losers are identified. We can't wait to see who's winning before we take action.

The holy grail of Silicon Valley entrepreneurs is the disruption of entire industries—because that's where the big money is to be made. Amazon dominates book retailing; Uber decimates taxi services; Pandora displaces radio. Little attention is paid to the resulting destruction of livelihoods and assets because there's no incentive to do so. And what's cooking in the research labs is quickening the hearts of investors everywhere.

My goal in this book is to equip you with the intellectual tools, ethical foundation, and psychological framework required to successfully navigate these challenges. Whether we wind up as desperate paupers, willing to gamble our last dime for a chance to join the haves on Easy Street or as freethinking artists, athletes, and academics tenderly cared for by our own creations will largely depend on the public policies we put in place over the next decade or two.

Of course, many talented and thoughtful writers have already rung the alarm about the risks of recent technological advances. Some have expressed this in the form of engaging stories;[3] others have brought to bear the analytical skills of economists.[4] My goal here is to add a different voice to the growing chorus of concern, mine from the perspective of a technology entrepreneur.

Despite this litany of plagues, I remain an optimist. I'm confident we can craft a future of eternal peace and unbounded prosperity. I truly believe the world will be *Star Trek,* not *Terminator.* In the end, the tsunami of new technology will sweep in an extraordinary era of freedom, convenience, and happiness, but it's going to be a rough ride if we don't keep our hands firmly on the wheel of progress.

Welcome to the future, which begins in the past.

# 1. Teaching Computers to Fish

y 1960, IBM realized it had a problem. At a conference four years earlier, in the summer of 1956, a group of leading academics convened to consider how to build machines that, as they put it, "simulated every aspect of human intelligence." The collection of brash young scientists brainstormed for two months among the stately Georgian spires and lush gardens of Dartmouth College, fueled by the bold prediction of the organizers that "a significant advance can be made in one or more of these problems if a carefully selected group of scientists work on it together for a summer."[1] They may not have agreed on much, but they unanimously adopted the moniker "artificial intelligence" for their endeavor, as suggested by their host, the mathematician John McCarthy. It was a heady time.

Returning to their respective institutions, few seemed to notice that the optimistic goals of the conference were largely unmet. But that didn't stop them from expressing their enthusiasm for the newly minted field. Their predictions were soon featured in general-interest publications such as *Scientific American* and the *New York Times*.[2]

Among the conference organizers was Nathaniel Rochester, a star researcher at IBM's Watson Research Lab, who was tapped to lead the company's nascent AI efforts. But as word spread about his team's work on computer programs that played chess and proved mathematical theorems, complaints started to mount from an unexpected source.

The singular focus of IBM's storied sales force was to sell the latest data-processing equipment to industry and government. Renowned for aggressive tactics and armed with an answer to every objection, the sales force began reporting back to headquarters that decision makers were concerned about just how far this new push into AI might go. It was one thing to replace lowly clerks who typed up memos and sent out bills, but quite another to suggest that the same computers IBM was urging them to buy might someday threaten their own jobs as managers and supervisors.

Rising to this challenge, an internal IBM report suggested that the company cease all research in AI and shutter Rochester's new department.[3] Perhaps concerned for their own jobs, members of IBM management not only implemented these recommendations but also armed their sales force with the simple riposte, "Computers can only do what they are programmed to do."[4]

This straightforward phrase may be one of the most widely circulated and potent cultural memes of the last half century. It deftly neutered concerns about the mysterious, brightly colored Pandora's boxes IBM was installing on raised floors in special air-conditioned "computer rooms" throughout the world. Nothing to fear here: these electronic brains are just obedient mechanical servants blindly following your every instruction!

Programmers schooled in sequential step-wise processing, in which you break a problem down into ever more manageable chunks (called "structured programming"), would be quick to agree, perhaps even today. Computers at the time were monolithic devices that loaded some data from a finite memory, fetched an instruction, operated on that data, then stored the result. Connecting two computers together (networking) was unheard of, much less having access to volumes of information generated and stored elsewhere. Most programs could be described as a sequence of "Do this, then do that" instructions. Rinse and repeat.

Despite the lofty goals of the field, AI programs of the time reinforced this paradigm. Following the orientation of the founders, many early AI efforts focused on stringing logical axioms together to reach conclusions, a form of mathematical proof. As a result, they tended to focus on domains that were amenable to logical analysis and planning, such as playing board games, proving theorems, and solving puzzles. The other advantage of these "toy" problems was that they didn't require access to large amounts of messy data about the real world, which was in scarce supply, to say the least.

In the context of the time, these efforts could be seen as an obvious next step in expanding the utility of computers. The machines were initially conceived as general-purpose calculators for tasks like building ballistics tables for the military during World War II; IBM had successfully beaten these electronic swords into plowshares by applying them not only to numbers but also to the processing of letters, words, and documents. AI researchers were simply further expanding the class of processed data to include symbols of any kind, whether preexisting or newly invented for specific purposes like playing chess. Ultimately, this style of AI came to be called the symbolic systems approach.

But the early AI researchers quickly ran into a problem: the computers didn't seem to be powerful enough to do very many interesting tasks. Formalists who studied the arcane field of theory of computation understood that building faster computers could not address this problem. No matter how speedy the computer, it could never tame what was called the "combinatorial explosion." Solving real-world problems through step-wise analysis had this nasty habit of running out of steam the same way pressure in a city's water supply drops when vast new tracts of land are filled with housing developments.

Imagine finding the quickest driving route from San Francisco to New York by measuring each and every way you could possibly go; your trip would never get started. And even today, that's not how contemporary mapping applications give you driving instructions, which is why you may notice that they don't always take the most efficient route.

Much of the next several decades of AI research could be characterized as attempts to address the issue that logically sound approaches to programming tended to quickly peter out as the problems got more complex. Great effort went into the study of heuristics, which could loosely be described as "rules of thumb" to pare down the problems to manageable size. Basically, you did as much searching for an answer as you could afford to, given the available computing power, but when push came to shove you would turn to rules that steered you away from wasting time on candidate solutions that were unlikely to work. This process was called pruning the search space.

Monumental debates broke out over where, exactly, the intelligence was in these programs. Researchers in "heuristic programming" soon came to realize that the answer lay not in the rote search for a solution or the process of stringing logical propositions together, but rather in the rules they used for pruning.

Most of these rules came from experts in the problem domain, such as chess masters or doctors. Programmers who specialized in interviewing experts to incorporate their skills into AI programs became known as "knowledge engineers," and the resulting programs were called "expert systems." While these programs were certainly a step in the right direction, very few of them turned out to be robust enough to solve practical real-world problems.

So the question naturally arose: What is the nature of expertise? Where does it come from, and could a computer program become an expert automatically? The obvious answer was that you needed lots of practice and exposure to relevant examples. An expert race car driver isn't born with the ability to push a vehicle to its operating limits, and a virtuoso isn't born holding a violin. But how could you get a computer program to learn from experience?

A small fringe group of AI researchers, right from the earliest days, thought that mimicking human brain functions might be a better way. They recognized that "Do this, then do that" was not the only way to program a computer, and it appeared that the brain took a different, more flexible approach. The problem was that precious little was known about the brain, other than that it contains lots of intricately interconnected cells called neurons, which appear to be exchanging chemical and electrical signals among themselves.

So the researchers simulated that structure in a computer, at least in a very rudimentary form. They made lots of copies of a program, similar in structure to a neuron, that accepted a bunch of inputs and produced an output, in a repeating cycle. They then networked these copies into layers by connecting the outputs of lower layers into the inputs of higher layers. The connections were often numeric weights, so a weight of zero might mean not connected and a weight of one hundred might mean strongly connected. The essence of these programs was the way they automatically adjusted their weights in response to example data presented to the inputs of the lowest layer of the network. The researcher simply presented as many examples as possible, then turned the crank to propagate these weights throughout the system until it settled down.[5]

Following the tendency for AI researchers to anthropomorphize, they called these programs "neural networks." But whether these programs actually functioned the way brains do was beside the point: it was simply a different approach to programming.

The most important difference between the symbolic systems and neural networking approaches to AI is that the former requires the programmer to predefine the symbols and logical rules that constitute the domain of discourse for the problem, while the latter simply requires the programmer to present sufficient examples. Rather than tell the computer *how* to solve the problem, you show it examples of *what* you want it to do. This sounds terrific, but in practice, it didn't work very well—at least initially.

One of the earliest neural networking efforts was by Frank Rosenblatt at Cornell in 1957, who called his programmatic neurons "perceptrons."[6] He was able to show that, with enough training, a network of his perceptrons could learn to recognize (classify) simple patterns in the input. The problem was, as with symbolic systems programs, the results were mainly small demonstrations on toy problems. So it was hard to assess the ultimate potential of this approach, not to mention that Rosenblatt's claims for his work rankled some of his friendly academic competitors, particularly at MIT.

Not to let this challenge go unanswered, two prominent MIT researchers published a widely read paper proving that, if limited in specific ways, a network of perceptrons was incapable of distinguishing certain inputs unless at least one perceptron at the lowest level was connected to every perceptron at the next level, a seemingly critical flaw.[7] The reality, however, was a little different. In practice, slightly more complex networks easily overcome this problem. But science and engineering don't always proceed rationally, and the mere suggestion that you could formally prove that perceptrons had limitations called the entire approach into question. In short order, most funding (and therefore progress) dried up.

At this point, readers close to the field are likely rolling their eyes that I'm retelling this shopworn history-in-a-bottle tale, which ends with the underdog winning the day: the 1990s and 2000s witnessed a resurgence of the old techniques, with increasingly persuasive results. Rebranded as machine learning and big data, and enhanced with advanced architectures, techniques, and use of statistics, these programs began to recognize objects in real photographs, words in spoken phrases, and just about any other form of information that exhibits patterns.[8]

But there's a deeper story here than researcher-gets-idea, idea-gets-quashed, idea-wins-the-day. There's an important reason why machine learning was so weak in the late twentieth century compared to symbolic systems, while the opposite is true today. Information technology in general, and computers in particular, changed. Not just by a little, not just by a lot, but so dramatically that they are essentially different beasts today than they were fifty years ago.

The scale of this change is so enormous that it's difficult to conjure up meaningful analogies. The term *exponential growth* is thrown around so often (and so imprecisely) that most people don't really understand what it means. It's easy to define—a quantity that changes in proportion to a fixed number raised to a changing power—but it's hard for the human mind to grasp what that means. The powers 100, 1,000, 10,000 (powers of 10), and 32, 64, 128 (powers of 2), are numeric examples. But these numbers can get mind-bogglingly large very quickly. In just eighty steps in the first of these example sequences, the figure is larger than the estimated number of atoms in the entire universe.

For at least the last half century, important measures of computing, such as processing speed, transistor density, and memory, have been doubling approximately every eighteen to twenty-four months, which is an exponential pace (power of 2). At the start of the computer revolution, no one could have predicted that the power of these machines would grow exponentially for such a sustained period. Gordon Moore, cofounder of Intel, noticed this trend as early as 1965, but remarkably, this pattern has continued unabated through today with only minor bumps along the way.[9] It could all end tomorrow, as indeed concerned industry watchers have warned for decades. But so far, progress marches on without respite.

You've probably experienced this remarkable achievement yourself without realizing it. Your first smartphone may have had a spacious eight gigabytes of memory, a small miracle for its time. Two years later, if you bothered to upgrade, you likely sprang for sixteen gigabytes of memory. Then thirty-two. Then sixty-four. The world didn't end, but consider that your phone contains eight times as much memory as it did three upgrades ago, for pretty much the same cost. If your car got eight times the gas mileage it did six years ago, on the order of, say, two hundred miles per gallon, you may have taken more notice.

Now project this forward. If you upgrade your phone every two years for the next ten years, it's not unreasonable to expect it to come with two terabytes (two thousand gigabytes). The equivalent improvement in gas mileage for your car would be over six thousand miles per gallon. You could drive from New York City to Los Angeles and back on one gallon, and still have enough left to make it down to Atlanta for the winter before refueling, with just another gallon.

Imagine how mileage like this would change things. Gas would effectively be free. Drilling for oil would come to a near standstill. Airlines and shipping companies would constantly scramble to adopt the latest hyperefficient motor technology. The cost of package delivery, freight, plane tickets, and consumer goods would drop significantly. This blistering rate of change is precisely what's happening in the computer industry, and the secondary effects are transforming businesses and labor markets everywhere.

So your phone might have two thousand gigabytes of storage. What does that mean? To put that in perspective, your brain contains about one hundred "giga-neurons." This is not to suggest that twenty bytes of computer memory is as powerful as a neuron, but you get the picture. It's quite possible, if not likely, that within a decade or two your smartphone may in principle have as much processing power as your brain. It's hard to even imagine today what we will do with all this power, and it's quite possibly just around the corner.

To my children, this story is just the ramblings of an old-timer talking about the good ol' days. But to me, this is personal. Over the 1980 winter holiday break at Stanford, I helped some researchers from SRI International build a program that could answer questions posed in English to a database. Though the system's linguistic capability was rudimentary compared to today's, the team leader, Gary Hendrix, was able to use this demo to raise venture capital funding for a new company that he cleverly named Symantec.

Sequestered in my basement for two solid weeks, I cobbled together a flexible database architecture to support the project. Gary had loaned me a state-of-the-art personal computer of the time, the Apple II. This remarkable machine stored information on floppy disks and supported a maximum of forty-eight thousand bytes of memory. To put this in perspective, that Apple II could store about one second of CD-quality music. By contrast, the phone I'm carrying around today, which has sixty-four gigabytes of memory, can hold about twelve days of CD-quality music. My phone literally has over 1 million times as much memory as that Apple II, for a fraction of the cost.

What does a factor of 1 million mean? Consider the difference between the speed at which a snail crawls and the speed of the International Space Station while in orbit. That's a factor of merely half a million. The computer on which I am typing these words has far more computing power than was available to the entire Stanford AI Lab in 1980.

While it's possible to compare the processing power and memory of today's and yesterday's computers, the advances in networking can't even be meaningfully quantified. In 1980, for all practical purposes, the concept barely existed. The Internet Protocol, the basis for what we now call IP addresses, wasn't even standardized until 1982.[10] Today, literally billions of devices are able to share data nearly instantly, as you demonstrate every time you make a phone call or send a text message. The enormous and growing mountain of data of nearly every kind, stored on devices accessible to you through the Internet, is astonishing.

So how did this affect the relative success of the various approaches to AI? At some point, large enough differences in quantity become qualitative. And the evolution of computers is clearly in this category, even though progress may seem gradual on a day-to-day basis, or from Christmas gift to Christmas gift. As you might expect, machines so vastly different in power may require different programming techniques. You don't race a snail the same way you would race a spaceship.

The original symbolic systems approach was tailored to the computers available at the time. Since there was precious little computer-readable data available at all, and no way to store any significant volume of it, researchers made do by handcrafting knowledge they painstakingly distilled from interviews with experts. The focus was on building efficient algorithms to search for a solution because the limited processing power would not permit anything more ambitious.

The alternative neural networking approach (more commonly called machine learning today), which attempted to learn from examples, simply required too much memory and data for early computers to demonstrate meaningful results. There were no sufficiently large sources of examples to feed to the programs, and even if you could, the number of "neurons" you could simulate was far too small to learn anything but the simplest of patterns.

But as time went by, the situation reversed. Today's computers can not only represent literally billions of neurons but, thanks to the Internet, they can easily access enormous troves of examples to learn from. In contrast, there's little need to interview experts and shoehorn their pearls of wisdom into memory modules and processors that are vanishingly small and slow compared to those available today.

Important subtleties of this technological revolution are easy to overlook. To date, there seem to be no limitations on just how expert machine learning programs can become. Current programs appear to grow smarter in proportion to the amount of examples they have access to, and the volume of example data grows every day. Freed from dependence on humans to codify and spoon-feed the needed insight, or to instruct them as to how to solve the problem, today's machine learning systems rapidly exceed the capabilities of their creators, solving problems that no human could reasonably be expected to tackle. The old proverb, suitably updated, applies equally well to machines as people: Give a computer some data, and you feed it for a millisecond; teach a computer to search, and you feed it for a millennium.[11]

In most cases, it's impossible for the creators of machine learning programs to peer into their intricate, evolving structure to understand or explain what they know or how they solve a problem, any more than I can look into your brain to understand what you are thinking about. These programs are no better able to articulate what they do and how they do it than human experts—they just know the answer. They are best understood as developing their own intuitions and acting on instinct: a far cry from the old canard that they "can only do what they are programmed to do."

I'm happy to report that IBM long ago came around to accepting the potential of AI and to recognizing its value to its corporate mission. In 2011, the company demonstrated its in-house expertise with a spectacular victory over the world's champion *Jeopardy!* player, Ken Jennings. IBM is now parlaying this victory into a broad research agenda and has, characteristically, coined its own term for the effort: cognitive computing. Indeed, it is reorganizing the entire company around this initiative.

It's worth noting that IBM's program, named Watson, had access to 200 million pages of content consuming four terabytes of memory.[12] As of this writing, three years later, you can purchase four terabytes of disk storage from Amazon for about $150. Check back in two years, and the price will likely be around $75. Or wait ten years, and it should set you back about $5. Either way, be assured that Watson's progeny are coming to a smartphone near you.

**2.** Teaching Robots to Heel

ossibly the first time a robot actually ran amok was in 1972 at a lab near Boston. Marvin Minsky, head of the MIT Artificial Intelligence Laboratory, had written a proposal suggesting that a doctor might someday be able to control a robot arm remotely to perform surgery. But he needed an actual computer-controlled arm to investigate the idea. So he called his friend John McCarthy at Stanford, who arranged to lend him a research assistant to help out with the project. Victor Scheinman, a young mechanical engineering whiz, quickly designed a prototype that was later to become the basis of one of the first commercially successful computer-controlled arms (the PUMA, for programmable universal manipulator for assembly).[1]

The theory was great, but the reality lagged behind. The arm was heavy, difficult to control, and had to be bolted to a table for stability. One day, probably due to a programming error, the arm started to oscillate back and forth. As it gained momentum, the table began to shake violently, then started to rock its way across the room with each swing of the arm. A hapless graduate student working in the lab didn't notice at first as the newly mobile robot approached. By the time he did, it was too late: he was trapped in a corner. He crouched down and cried for help as his mechanical tormentor relentlessly approached. Just before he was to become a historical footnote, a coworker rushed in to halt the control computer and bring the rampage to an end.[2]

The tendency to think of AI systems in general and robots in particular as analogs of human brains and brawn is understandable, but it carries significant dangers. The field has a long history of exploiting our natural tendency to anthropomorphize objects that look or act like us in order to attract attention and increase funding. But it also misleads people into believing that machines are more like us than they really are, and into assuming that they are capable of understanding and abiding by our social conventions. Without a deep understanding of *how* these systems work, and with humans as the only available exemplars with which to interpret the results, the temptation to view them as humanlike is irresistible. But they aren't.

IBM's *Jeopardy!*-playing Watson is a recent example. There was really no technical reason to have the system "say" its responses in a calm, didactic tone of voice, much less to put up a headlike graphic of swirling lights suggesting that the machine had a mind that was thinking about the problem. These were incidental adornments to a tremendous technical achievement. Few observers even realized that Watson wasn't listening to the *Jeopardy!* clues at all: the text was transmitted instantly when Alex Trebek began talking, giving the computer an enormous head start in "computer time" while the human contestants had to wait for him to finish. But Watson's main advantage was its ability to "ring in" quickly, pressing the answer button milliseconds after receiving a signal that the clue was complete, far faster than humanly possible. The IBM program could just as well have been described as a very sophisticated data-retrieval system and given a more technical-sounding name, but that just wouldn't have had the same television curb appeal.

The gratuitous anthropomorphism plaguing the field, which I refer to as "AI theater," extracts a hidden cost. Like calling the Internet "cyberspace," which implies that it is somehow a separate domain exempt from our laws and regulations, it muddies public understanding and therefore hampers important policy issues and debates.

So it's not surprising that when robots with humanlike mechanical appendages began appearing on factory floors, it was tempting for people to expect them to behave with some semblance of human social restraint, such as not lashing out and striking people randomly. Besides, as everyone knew, they could only do what they were programmed to do.

The problem is that these early robots typically just repeated rote motions on cue. If you got in their way, you were in serious danger of getting whacked, or worse. It quickly became clear that OSHA (Occupational Safety and Health Administration) rules regarding factory floor safety must treat these robots as a new class of enhanced machines, not as dumbed-down workers. In factories and research labs, including the one at MIT, the standard practice was to place brightly colored tape on the floor around a robot, indicating a "kill zone" inside of which you were forbidden to venture without special precautions. Giant red OFF buttons, of the sort commonly depicted in movies, were placed in strategic locations in case of an emergency.

Industrial robots have evolved significantly over the decades, but most of the advances have been in the precision of their control, strength, and durability as well as reduced weight and cost. As a general matter, their working environments have to be designed around them, rather than the other way around. Because they typically can't see, hear, or otherwise sense their surroundings, those surroundings have to be simple and predictable. If an industrial robot arm is expecting a bolt to be in a particular position at a particular moment, it damn well better be exactly where it's supposed to be or the entire process has to be restarted. They can't beg for mulligans on the factory floor, as novice players do in golf.

Your kitchen dishwasher is designed the way it is for the same reason. Each dish and cup must be placed with care for a rotating arm that sprays soap and water around blindly and indiscriminately. You must accommodate to the robot's needs because it can't conform to yours.

Because I was trained to steer clear of these mechanical death traps, I was quite surprised, upon returning to the Stanford AI Lab, to find a graduate student having a mock swordfight with a robot.[3] Not only did the mechanical fencer track its opponent's moves and plan its own motions, it could stop just short of potentially lethal actions. When I was invited to do so, it was quite an experience for me to guide the robot's arms into various poses, which it would dutifully hold until I directed it to change, like a marionette without strings.

What made this possible is a confluence of four advancing technologies. I've already discussed the first two—vast increases in computing power and progress in machine learning techniques. The third is improvements in the industrial design of robots. New designs use lighter-weight materials and more sophisticated control mechanisms, so their products have far less ability to cause damage and can respond instantly when unexpected obstacles are encountered (such as a human head).

But the real breakthroughs are in the field of machine perception. Until the past decade or so, progress has been slow and steady in programs that interpret visual images. But the application of machine learning techniques, combined with increasingly sophisticated and inexpensive cameras, has led to a sudden acceleration of capabilities. Programs can now examine pictures and videos to rapidly recognize objects, people, and actions, and describe them with high accuracy ("a group of young people playing a game of Frisbee").[4] You may already see a primitive example of this when your camera identifies the presence of faces in its viewfinder.

The same basic techniques can be applied to all sorts of sensors, of course. Systems can identify songs by their sound, classify ships at sea based on radar and sonar soundings, even diagnose cardiac ailments using EKG or ultrasound readings.

A potent cocktail of these four technologies is going to change everything. Once again, we lack adequate reference points to properly anchor our understanding, but a good place to start is with forged laborers. Today's preprogrammed, repetitive mechanical devices are primitive precursors to robots that can see, hear, plan, and adapt their behavior to chaotic and complex real-world situations. These are robots that, quite simply, will be able to accomplish many, if not most, tasks that currently require human manual labor.

You can buy a robot that can vacuum your floors. And already in commercial development are robots that can weed a garden, load and unload randomly shaped boxes from delivery trucks, follow you around carrying your bags, and pick crops. In fact, they can even selectively harvest only the fruit that is ripe and ready.[5] Soon, just about every physical task you can imagine will be subject to automation: painting exterior and interior spaces, cooking meals, busing dishes, cleaning tables, serving food, making beds, folding laundry, walking dogs, laying pipe, washing sidewalks, fetching tools, taking tickets, sewing, and directing traffic, just to name a small number of consumer-facing examples.

And this doesn't begin to touch on the industrial applications, such as picking and packing orders, stocking and straightening shelves, welding and cutting, polishing, inspecting, assembling, sorting, even repairing other robotic devices. Then there are the military applications, some of which are unbearably nightmarish. (For example, within the next decade or so just about anyone—including extremists worldwide—is likely to be able to field a swarm of solar-powered human-seeking robotic insects that can shimmy through door jams and ventilation shafts to deliver a painless dose of lethal poison, then retrace their tracks to save the inconvenience of manual retrieval. Add an optional face-recognition pack and get targeted assassinations for the same low price!) As our comfort grows with these sophisticated devices, we will permit them into more intimate settings, to do tasks such as cutting our hair and giving massages. Robotic prostitutes (which I will discuss in chapter 8) are not far off, and may very well be one of the earliest and most lucrative markets.

But it's important to understand that the various components of this remarkable trend are not confined to our common conception of a robot. While some of these devices may be self-contained, like the milquetoast humanoid C3P0 or the mechanical factotum R2D2, there's no reason such systems must have what's called in the trade "locality." That is, they need not be confined to exist in or operate on a particular contiguous expanse of physical space. In other words, they may not be embodied, in the conventional sense of the word.

You may wonder why you are you and not me, as opposed to why you and I aren't two parts of the same organism. That may sound odd, but I suspect it seems less peculiar to conjoined twins who share one heart and digestive system.

Performing any given task requires certain resources and capabilities. These resources fall roughly into four categories: energy (so you can do work), awareness (the ability to sense the relevant aspects of the environment), reasoning (so you can formulate and adjust a plan), and means (so you can actually get something done, like picking up an object with your hands). In principle, none of these resources have to be colocated. In practice, it's often useful that they are.

You are an example. Because biological creatures by themselves can't communicate or transmit energy over long distances (as far as we know), all their body parts have to be near each other. The cells that make up your body communicate with biochemical and electrical impulses transmitted through various conduits and nerves. So there's a good design reason that your eyes (awareness) are near your brain (reasoning), and your feet are found at the ends of your legs (means). Not to mention that there's one engine to power all of this, extracting resources from your food (energy).

About 120 years ago, after millions of years of evolution, something magical happened: through us, life suddenly developed the means to burst free of the locality constraint. Guglielmo Marconi figured out how to use electromagnetic radiation—more commonly called radio waves—to transmit information instantly between distant locations with no evident physical connection. And Thomas Edison figured out how to move energy, in the form of electricity, through wires at a relatively low cost.

We're still sorting out what this will ultimately mean.[6] My personal view is that the entire history of electrical engineering, electronics, radio, television, the Internet, computers, and AI to date is merely our initial awkward attempts to explore what can be done with these newly discovered phenomena. But one thing's for sure: as slowly evolving biological creatures, we aren't the best actors to exploit them. Machines are.

Shortly after birth, we start to understand the world by parsing it up into objects, which we soon begin to separate into animate and inanimate varieties. We have a special affinity for the animate objects most like us: other people. Many of our highest social instincts, such as love and sympathy, can be understood as nature's way of encouraging us to take a view broader than our own immediate interests. If you're concerned only with your next meal, why not bite the hand that feeds you?

Seeing your surroundings as a collection of objects is a good way to organize your world when the things that matter most to your immediate survival are within earshot and have clear physical boundaries. It's much harder to understand things that are invisible, fast moving, and diffuse, like a radiation cloud or your reputation on the Internet. Our highways are littered with corpses of creatures whose senses aren't attuned to detecting two-ton metallic threats speeding down the road. Likewise, we don't even have the vocabulary yet to discuss the technological changes bearing down on us, as I can attest in grasping for the best terms to use in this book. As a result, we are in danger of becoming roadkill on the so-called information superhighway.

But how will robots experience the world differently? There's no need for their eyes and ears (or appropriate alternatives) to be mounted on their bodies. Quite the contrary, they would be better off with a network of sensors distributed throughout the environment of interest. Your depth perception and ability to locate sounds would be far better if you could separate your ears and eyes by yards instead of inches, not to mention if you could add additional ones at will facing in various directions. Consider, for instance, how much better the automated ShotSpotter system is at locating gunshots than the police are.

Similarly, there's no reason for the means by which robots pursue their goals to be bound together in one package. They can consist of a collection of disconnected and interchangeable actuators, motors, and tools. Finally, the logic that coordinates and drives all of this can be anywhere, like the remote drone pilots in the Nevada desert unleashing Hellfire missiles in Afghanistan.

Free of the inconvenient constraints of locality, what will robots look like to us? Unfortunately, because of our natural history, the answer is not much.

Consider a robotic housepainter. It's easy to imagine a humanoid form climbing ladders and swinging a brush alongside its mortal coworkers. But it's more likely to appear (for instance) as a squadron of flying drones, each outfitted with a spray nozzle and trailing a bag of paint. The drones maintain a precise distance from each other and the wood siding of your Colonial, instantly adjusting for wind gusts and other factors. As they individually run low on supplies, they fly over to a paint barrel to automatically refill and recharge, then return to the most useful open position. A series of cameras sprinkled around the perimeter of the project continuously monitors this flying menagerie and assesses the progress and quality of the job. The actual device directing this mechanical ballet needn't even be present. It can be what's called software-as-a-service (SAAS) rented by the manufacturer and running on the Amazon cloud.[7] Why bother to put all that computing power out in the field where it may get rained on and be used only a few hours a week?

Your licensed painting contractor, who might still be paying off the loan for all this fancy gear, shows up, sets up the cameras, marks the target area on an app running on his tablet, opens the paint barrel, and turns on the drones. An entire house could be painted in an afternoon instead of a week, at a fraction of today's cost. In the system's first incarnation, workers may still prep the surfaces and lay drop cloths, but soon that won't be necessary as product engineers upgrade the system and add components.

This may sound like science fiction, but it's not. All the technologies required to do this are available now. It's simply a matter of some resourceful entrepreneur making it happen. (Go for it!)

There are, of course, lots of tasks we would like to perform that are much more geographically diverse than painting a house. Imagine an army of solar-powered, heat-seeking mobile wildfire extinguishers, capable of rolling their way around the forest floor, strategically positioned in potential hotspots and directed by a server at the National Forest Service.

Looking further to the future while staying rooted in today's technologies, imagine the fire extinguishers, shrunk to the size of insects, digging themselves into miniature foxholes awaiting a command to spring into action. When summoned, they might self-assemble to form a protective dome or blanket around homes, infrastructure, even individual people. Research on concepts like this is active enough to have earned the name "swarm robotics."

Even self-driving cars aren't going to be nearly as self-contained or autonomous as they appear. Standards for vehicles and roadside sensors to share information wirelessly, essentially becoming one interconnected system of eyes and ears, are close to completion. The U.S. Department of Transportation, among other institutions, is developing so-called V2V (vehicle to vehicle) communications protocols by piggybacking on the Federal Communications Commission's allocation of radio spectrum for dedicated short-range communications (DSRC) specifically intended for automotive applications. Integrated with traffic control and energy management systems, your future car will simply be the visible manifestation of an integrated flexible public transportation system, centrally monitored and managed, the same way your cell phone is best understood as an element in an enormous communication system. The magic is no more in your car or your phone than TV shows are located in your TV.

As sensors, effectors, and wireless communications continue to improve, they will vanish from view as surely as computer technology has. I'm old enough to recall a day when you could pick up a piece of computer memory and literally see each bit (called "core memories"). Today, we perceive gigabytes of computer memory as flat, black rectangles the size of a postage stamp, if they are physically separable from other components at all. Someday you may be walking through what looks like a pristine wilderness, blissfully unaware that an extensive network of self-organizing, collaborative devices are maintaining the environment and watching out for you (or watching you!) as though you were visiting Disneyland.

Finally, many arenas involve only the manipulation of information, such as our financial systems, educational institutions, and entertainment media. The energy, awareness, reasoning, and means to perform useful work may be entirely available in the electronic domain, requiring no locality at all. Needed data may be collected instantly from around the world, tasks may be shifted at will, and actions taken wherever most convenient (for instance, where a stock exchange happens to be open).

The point is that while we may think of robots as objects and of programs as a series of written instructions, they are really just different manifestations of the same phenomenon: the power of electricity to perform work and process information. We aren't designed to perceive this new magic in action, but we're still subject to its effects.

Another inevitable trend may seem counterintuitive: the tendency for technologies to coalesce and simplify. Whereas biological creatures proliferate and differentiate from one another in a branching "tree of life," their mechanical counterparts do the exact opposite.

Consider, for instance, your mobile phone. In the past, you may have owned a GPS for your car, a camera, a VCR, a CD player, not to mention an actual cell phone. Today, these gadgets and their markets have nearly disappeared, displaced by a single economical device, the modern electronic equivalent of a Swiss army knife, because their shared technological components are very similar.

Returning to the wild, the National Guard could quickly realize that the firefighting system described above could also be used for search and rescue missions, with the autonomous extinguishers serving as mechanical St. Bernards. Then the Coast Guard could replace the extinguishers with swimming robotic lifeguards that recharge by capturing wave motion. And so on.

The typical (and misguided) conception of the future is one filled with magical special-purpose contraptions to do every little thing, when in fact the opposite will be true. Cabinets in my kitchen are littered with seldom-used tools, each designed to do one thing well: brew coffee, heat soup, cook rice, pop popcorn, churn ice cream, roast hot dogs, toast bread, open cans, make juice, poach eggs—and these are only the ones that need electricity. The remaining cabinets hold an incredible variety of handheld tools and cooking utensils, ranging from a garlic press to a corkscrew. Not to mention the larger appliances that wash dishes, preserve food, make ice, compact trash, and cook.

Imagine a single forged laborer replacing them all. If it needs to dice some onions, it could fetch the needed component from its box of optional attachments. It could stand all day and wash dishes—no need to place them into the specialized racks of that dumb device with rotating arms that wastes soap and water. And between meals, it could shell sunflower seeds, make ice cream, polish silverware, and tenderize steak. But why stop there? It could also clean the floors, make the beds, and eventually change the baby's diaper. If the weather permits, why not have it plant and grow food in the backyard?

Such a forged laborer could perform all of these functions with nothing more than the primitive equipment available to a medieval cook. Which is the point: the future looks a lot more like the past than you might expect. Our lives may be more complex, but they will appear simpler than they do today, surrounded by invisible technologies controlling an unassuming collection of versatile, adaptable devices. The coming wave of forged laborers will literally sweep the factory floor and do your chores. You can cart your old dishwasher to the junkyard.

The current trend toward technological complexity and diversity is a temporary diversion—a modern-day Cambrian explosion fueled by electricity but destined to settle down into mechanical phyla yet to take shape.

It's relatively easy to understand how distributed mechanical systems that perform physical labor will mutate and expand to fill niches in our homes, businesses, and environment. But it's much harder to see that the same trends are unfolding in our commercial, intellectual, and social environments. Amazon replaces everything from bookstores to shoe stores by combining the common functions into one unified system. Google replaces libraries, newspapers, and business directories under a single organizing umbrella. Facebook combines everything from postcards, photo sharing, invitations, thank-you notes, tips from friends, and high-fives into a seamless social piano roll.

While our minds are organized to pay attention to things we can point to, the things we can't see can be just as dangerous. Paradoxically, our evolving technologies are proliferating and consolidating at the same time, and we are ill suited to track, much less predict, the consequences. The trends described above—flexible robotic systems, capable of independent action, broadly distributed, spanning both physical and electronic domains, communicating at superhuman speeds and distances, shrinking into invisibility and magically self-organizing as necessary—will be as easy to miss but as hard to ignore as viruses. In the words of William Butler Yeats, "And what rough beast, its hour come round at last, / Slouches towards Bethlehem to be born?"[8]

**3.** Robotic Pickpockets

omputers are improving and engineers have new ways to program them. Big deal. So what? You'll care the first time you get mugged by a robot—and there's a good chance you already have been without realizing it.

In 1980, a Stanford graduate-student friend of mine named Dave Shaw was getting a bit anxious about his Ph.D. written exam. I told him that, in my experience, it was a good idea to study hard, but then take the final day off before the test to relax. So we went to see *Raiders of the Lost Ark* at the Palo Alto Square Theater.[1] After acing his exams and completing his thesis, he accepted a position as an assistant professor of computer science at Columbia University.

When I visited him a few years later, he was working on a remarkable project: a new design for computers that could speed up processing by breaking down linear, sequential computations into smaller tasks that could be performed simultaneously by multiple processors, then combined into a unified answer.[2] His goal for the project was to improve the processing of database queries. (This basic concept is known today as "MapReduce.")[3]

By 1986, it became clear to Dave that the paltry scale of government research grants, the lifeblood of academics and researchers, would be insufficient to realize his vision. So he headed south, from Morningside Heights to Wall Street. The powers that be at

Morgan Stanley, a leading investment banking firm both then and now, liked what they saw. They offered him a job reportedly at six times his professorial salary.[4] Morgan Stanley needed Shaw's technology for a new secretive business initiative to use computers to buy and sell stocks. By then, computers were common on Wall Street to *process* stock transactions, but not to *pick* which stocks to buy and sell. That was something that only people could do because, as everyone knew, computers can only do what they are programmed to do. But the prescient people at Morgan Stanley knew better.

Not only could developers design algorithms to buy and sell stocks, it became clear that a computer could trade much faster than a human. Morgan Stanley soon realized that moving the decision making from the physical world to the electronic provided decisive advantages as long as you made the right trades at the right time.

Today, programmatic buying and selling is known as HFT (high-frequency trading). How high frequency? If you press a button to buy a stock, then as quickly as you can press the button again to sell the stock, you could probably complete the pair of transactions in about one-tenth of a second. Today's HFT systems can complete approximately one hundred thousand transactions in about the same amount of time. Shaw's expertise designing superfast computers was just the ticket.

Joining Morgan Stanley opened Dave's eyes to a more fundamental truth. Trading quicker than the next guy was an advantage, but the real edge came from rapidly analyzing the torrent of data flowing through the world's financial markets—and Morgan Stanley had a riverside seat.

This insight wasn't unique. AI researchers back at Stanford, among many other centers of excellence, were coming to the same conclusion: the action was in the data, not the programs. And everyone involved realized that statistical and machine learning techniques were currently the best tools available to pan for gold. While his former colleagues began scrounging around for whatever real-world data they could get their hands on, Dave had accidentally perched himself on top of the mother lode. As he was quoted in a *Fortune* magazine article a decade later, "Finance is really a wonderfully pure information-processing business."[5]

Dave soon became disenchanted with his new patrons. I can only speculate that their notion of what the computers should do was rooted in the way human traders made their decisions, while Dave had a better idea: let the mathematicians and computer scientists run wild applying statistical and AI techniques to anything that moved. Barely eighteen months after joining Morgan Stanley, he took the courageous step of leaving to start his own investment bank, D. E. Shaw and Company, ultimately earning the admiring Wall Street moniker King Quant. His bosses probably thought he was nuts.

Because the actual techniques he (and others) employed are notoriously shrouded in secrecy, this is usually where the story dissolves into smoke and mirrors, only to focus on newly minted fortunes and grand mansions in the Hamptons. But let's take a somewhat closer look.[6]

As everyone knows, the way to make money in the stock market is to buy low and sell high (though not necessarily in that order). The first order of business in HFT was to find places where what was supposed to be a single price for some stock or commodity wasn't. In a term that Dave would recognize, data in this form is called *unnormalized*. You experience unnormalized data every day when you shop around for the lowest price. In principle, if information flowed freely, there would be only one price for the same item everywhere you looked, hopefully the best one possible.

Now, the simplest form of HFT is to notice when the same security can be bought or sold on one exchange at a different price than on another exchange. The prices are supposed to be the same, but this isn't always the case. The actual values jitter around from moment to moment, based on the vagaries of who happens to be selling how much on which market at any particular instant. When prices momentarily diverge, an HFT program can simultaneously purchase at the lower price while selling at the higher price, pocketing the "spread" without taking any risk.

These slight perturbations don't matter to human traders, because they can't react quickly enough to take advantage of the transient fluctuations. But computers can. So an HFT program can pick off a fraction of a cent in less than a blink of an eye, before prices inevitably normalize. In fact, the very act of buying and selling causes the prices to converge. Do this one hundred thousand times a second, across worldwide markets, and you're talking about serious money.

But the opportunity to collect free money is much larger and more nuanced. Like laundry detergent, securities come packaged in slightly different forms for slightly different purposes. For instance, you can buy a Treasury bill that will return your money in thirty years, or you can buy one that will return your money in twenty years. In principle, the current value of these two maturities should be closely related through a simple, predictable formula. But sometimes it isn't, and often for just a fraction of a second. If you detect the anomaly and bet on its impending resolution, you can collect a quick payout.

Add to this the fact that you don't have to be right all the time, just more of the time than you are wrong. While any individual transaction may entail some level of risk, the laws of probability ensure that, in aggregate, if your trades are tipped in your favor, you are guaranteed to make a profit. The house always wins.

Now apply this to markets everywhere. Plenty of individual prices that seem to be independent are actually correlated. If there's a drought in Southeast Asia, the price of sugar may rise, affecting the cost of chocolate in Sweden. But be careful—this might be offset by a drop in the price of cocoa beans in South America. Human traders endeavor to become expert in these matters, but no one comes close to the ability of a synthetic intellect to observe broad or subtle patterns.

One of my favorite examples is that the number of prepaid cell phone cards purchased is an indicator of the size of certain crops in Africa, because the individual farmers, watching their crops grow, are preparing to contact potential buyers. The more optimistic they are, the more they spend on talk minutes. The latest foray in this arena uses what's called "sentiment analysis." Yes, that kind of sentiment—programs at investment banks scour the Internet for positive or negative comments about products and companies, then trade on the information.

The typical justification proffered for doing all this is that HFT programs are providing a service to society. They are simply cleaning up inefficiencies in the markets. But this whitewashes a darker truth. Yes, they make the financial markets nice and tidy, but they obscure a deeper cost. They pollute the river of money by shifting risk to others, just as cheap detergents foul our waterways. What risk? That you aren't going to get the best price available when you go to buy or sell because someone stepped into the middle of your transaction.

In principle, the market-smoothing functions of HFT programs could be handled by public-interest systems that notified buyers and sellers that a better price was to be had elsewhere, so each could benefit from the value of this information. Instead, all the benefits accrue to the creators and operators of these systems. Indeed, the parties that should be motivated to address this problem are the exchanges themselves, but they thrive on high volumes of transactions. So anyone or anything that trades at a furious pace is good for business. Many retailers provide "low price" guarantees to encourage buyers to purchase immediately rather than shopping around. Why shouldn't this same courtesy extend to securities?

To put HFT programs in perspective, imagine that an enthusiastic entrepreneur in your town invented an invisible robot that followed people around, and when someone accidentally dropped a coin on the ground without noticing, it would silently scarf it up. The entrepreneur might persuade the city manager to permit deployment on the theory that it helps keep the sidewalks clean. And sure enough, the sidewalks would be cleaner. But wouldn't it better serve the public interest if the robot simply handed some or all of the money back instead of pocketing it for the entrepreneur?

A simple step to reduce the financial impact of HFT programs would be to charge a tiny amount for requests for information, that is, bid and ask (price) requests.[7] Historically, a person requested a current "quote" by hand, so the number of inquiries was naturally limited. But computer-generated requests have changed all that. An HFT program might make millions of quote requests for each trade it executes. If the typical trade only netted one cent, but each quote cost one-thousandth of a cent, this would be a money-losing proposition.[8]

A second approach would be to delay *all* trades for one second, whether human or electronic. This increases the individual transaction risk just a smidge, because you can't be sure that transactions already queued ahead of you won't slightly change the price at which yours is executed. (In the analogy, you can't be sure that some other robot hasn't already picked the coin up, leaving you empty-handed.)[9] For human-generated transactions, this additional risk is vanishingly small. But relative to the expected value of an HFT transaction, it can loom large. A short artificial delay might also slow or stop the incredible arms race currently under way to reduce transaction latency.[10] This would go a long way toward eliminating the worst abuses by cutting the tail off the HFT opportunity.

Government regulators love the clean, well-oiled markets that HFT programs tidy up. But they are oblivious, indeed deferential, to the immense transfer of wealth that results. A ride through the wealthy counties north of New York City tells the story. Graceful estates surround quaint towns populated largely by partners at investment banking firms and hedge funds. Indeed, Dave Shaw is building a thirty-eight-thousand-square-foot manse in Hastings-on-Hudson at an estimated cost of $75 million.[11] Meanwhile, a candy bar at the East Harlem Target checkout costs a fraction of a cent extra. Who's to know or care?

It's important to understand that the practitioners of this rarified art aren't villains. They are simply applying their prodigious intellect and skills to the craft that our society has deemed most worthy of material reward. Despite the endless conga line of genuine Wall Street con artists and crooks whom ambitious public prosecutors parade before the cameras, the overwhelming majority of investment bankers are decent people making a living the best they can. I can personally assure you that Dave Shaw is foremost among them. A more diligent, thoughtful, and talented individual is hard to find in any profession. His philanthropic contributions, not to mention the pioneering hands-on research he is currently doing on protein folding at the research institute that bears his name, make him nothing less than a national treasure.[12]

The putative purpose of the stock exchanges is not to make some people rich but to facilitate commerce by allocating the flow of capital to its best and highest use. But the synthetic intellects that dominate today's markets call that mission into question.

Nathan Mayer Rothschild, seventeenth-century patriarch of the storied banking family, took this civic responsibility very seriously: he not only financed the Duke of Wellington's march against Napoleonic aggression (among many other public endeavors) but, contrary to legend, held back after receiving early notice of the duke's victory at Waterloo until the news was widely received by other investors, so as not to roil the markets.

In today's interconnected world, we can't afford to rely on the good graces and largess of prominent citizens. The committees and boards that manage our most important financial institutions lack Rothschild's discretion. Instead they are duty bound to serve the interests of their stockholders. As I will argue later, modest changes to our regulatory framework can set things back on the right track.

But there's more trouble brewing in paradise, and it's coming to a computer near you.

# 4. The Gods Are Angry

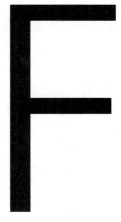or a glimpse of the future, consider what happened the lazy afternoon of May 6, 2010. By that time, the percentage of securities trades initiated by HFT programs had ballooned to an astonishing 60 percent.[1] For all practical purposes, machines, not people, populated markets. Your innocent E*Trade order for one hundred shares of Google was a mere snowflake in this perpetual blizzard, executed mainly as a courtesy to perpetuate the illusion that you can participate in the American dream.

Starting at precisely 2:42 p.m., the Dow Jones Industrial Average plunged in a matter of minutes, off more than a thousand points, or 9 percent, from its opening that day. Over $1 trillion in asset value had disappeared by 2:47. That's real money—your and my savings, retirement accounts, and school endowments. The stunned traders on exchange floors around the world could hardly believe their eyes. It was as if God himself had taken a hammer to the market. Surely this was some sort of horrible mistake?

It wasn't. It was the result of legitimate HFT programs doing exactly what they were designed to do.

It took the SEC (U.S. Securities and Exchange Commission) nearly six months to sort through the electronic wreckage and figure out what had transpired. While the commission's conclusions are somewhat controversial, which itself is an interesting commentary on what happened, the problem started when a money manager at a large mutual fund company (reportedly Waddell & Reed of

61

Overland, Kansas) placed an order to sell a sizable quantity of stock in a highly diversified form known as the S&P 500 E-Mini.[2] Ironically, Waddell & Reed is the antithesis of a quick-buck artist. Quite the contrary, it's known for an investing style called "fundamental analysis," buying and selling stocks slowly and methodically based on the performance of the underlying companies.

The hapless money manager wasn't trying to do anything unconventional. He simply placed a substantial but otherwise routine order to sell seventy-five thousand contracts as soon as practical, at a rate not to exceed 9 percent of the trading volume over the past minute, in an attempt to ensure smooth execution of the order. Then he turned his attention to other matters.

The problem was that there weren't enough buyers in the market for that particular security at that particular moment and, with nobody watching, prices dropped precipitously. As momentum built, and other programs automatically executed "stop-loss" orders to sell at any price, the denominator of that percentage grew and grew.

But that's only the start of the story. Safety alarms, responsibly incorporated into HFT programs all over the world, went off. Detecting unusual market fluctuations, some began dutifully unwinding positions at a furious pace to protect their patron's money. It was a full-on instant electronic bank run. The more aggressive ones, sensing a rare opportunity, smelled blood in the water. Interpreting the frantic buying and selling of their electronic counterparts as prey on the run, they traded furiously on their proprietary algorithms' predictions that the generous spreads would quickly evaporate. Due to the unprecedented volume of transactions, reporting systems fell behind, injecting false information into this pileup. Apple's stock price inexplicably soared to over $100,000 per share, while Accenture crashed to the bargain basement everything-must-go price of 1¢ per share. Really. Meanwhile, back in the real world, the sun was still shining and both companies were peaceably going about their business as usual.

In a moment as dramatic as a Hollywood cliffhanger, a single unassuming party saved the day with a simple action. The Chicago Mercantile Exchange, an out-of-town sideshow to the dominant market makers in New York, simply stopped all trading for a fleeting five seconds. That's right, a little longer than it will take you to read this sentence. A flash to you and me, but an eternity for the rampaging programs brawling as ferociously as they could. That was sufficient time for the markets to take a breath and for the HFT programs to reset. As soon as the mayhem ended, the usual market forces returned and prices quickly recovered to near where they had started just a few short minutes ago. The life-threatening tornado evaporated just as suddenly and inexplicably as it had appeared.

While the story may seem to have a happy ending, it does not. Confidence in the institutions we trust to shepherd our hard-earned savings is the bedrock of our financial system. No blue-ribbon presidential panel or SEC press release can restore this loss of faith. It can and will happen again, and that threat hangs over our every spending and savings decision. Investors can no longer go to sleep secure in the knowledge that when they awake, their nest egg will still be intact and incubating. The sorry truth is that its fate is in the hands of the machines.

These electronic wars aren't confined to the financial sector. They are becoming a standard part of our commercial landscape in a wide variety of areas. But you don't have to worry about them spilling over into your home. They already have, though in a more benign way.

On an unseasonably cool winter afternoon in Silicon Valley, I visited a friend who works at a hot new company called Rocket Fuel. Flush with a fresh infusion of $300 million from a secondary offering, Mark Torrance, chief technology officer, took a break to meet with me and discuss his company's business. His own customers have virtually no idea how he does what he does, but they certainly like the results. No, the company does not make fuel for rockets—it buys space on websites and display ads for household names like Toshiba, Buick, and Lord & Taylor. Sounds simple enough, until you consider how it's done. The company describes itself as a "Big Data and artificial intelligence company focused on digital marketing."[3]

You might wonder who decides which ads you see when you load a web page on your computer. You may assume that the owner of the website sells the space to the advertiser, possibly through an intermediary, like Rocket Fuel. But the truth is far more complex.

When you load a web page that contains ads, a monumental battle ensues behind the scenes in a snap of the fingers between a menagerie of exotic synthetic intellects. In the second or so between the time you click on a link and the page actually appears on your screen, hundreds of transactions ricochet around the Internet furiously gathering an astounding array of details about your recent behavior, estimating the likelihood that you can be influenced by one of the available advertisers, and engaging in a flash electronic auction for the right to make an impression on you. (Each display of a single ad is, in fact, called an "impression.") Rocket Fuel is one of the most heavily armed warriors in this electronic skirmish.

Let's start with the groundwork. Just about every time you

visit a website, click on a link, or type in a URL, the page that you load notifies one or more parties other than the site you are visiting of your arrival. How this is done isn't terribly important, but it does illustrate how the historical academic roots of the Internet have been repurposed for commercial purposes.

You may be aware that a web page actually contains links not only to other pages but also to files that display the pictures you see within the boundaries of the page, or "frame." When pages are slow to load, you may notice these separate links flash by briefly, usually in a status line at the bottom of your browser window. They may come from the same website that you are visiting, but they often come from elsewhere on the Internet. Each picture has specific dimensions, usually measured in pixels, short for "picture element." A pixel is basically one dot in a picture, with a color and brightness. So the more pixels in an image, the larger and/or more detailed the picture is. (You may have encountered this term in the form of "megapixels," or millions of pixels, which is used to tout the quality of digital camera images.)

Early in the development of the Internet, someone made the clever observation that a picture on a web page could contain a single pixel, making it essentially invisible to you. Why display this if you can't see it? That's the whole point. You can't see it, but that single pixel may come from anywhere, in particular from someone who would like to take note of when and from where you visited that particular page. Because the pixel comes from someone else's server, they get the automatic right to make a notation, usually on your hard drive. These notations are tiny files that go by the colorful moniker of "cookies." You can prevent this from happening with a setting in your browser, of course. But almost nobody does because it makes it hard to use lots of common features of websites. Also, the obscure web browser option to "block third-party cookies" means nothing to most people. Sounds like someone is withholding a tasty snack.

So what's in these cookies? Usually nothing but a unique identifier in the form of a big number. The important information is kept on the server of the party depositing the cookie. They would never entrust such valuable information to you because you might inadvertently share it with one of their competitors. You can think of this identifier as the electronic equivalent of gently sticking a Post-it note on your back so they can tell if they ever see you again.

And see you again they do, as you move around the Internet, browsing websites, clicking on links, reading articles, and buying products, because these parties have put pixels all over the place. As a result, they can construct a remarkably comprehensive profile of your habits—what you like and don't like, where you live, what you buy and from whom, whether you travel, what ailments you may suffer from, what you read, watch, and eat. But as extensive as this portrait is, it omits one crucial detail: who you actually are. They can construct a detailed picture of a single individual without knowing that person's name, face, or other identifying details except that you are using a particular computer.

Now, you might wonder why the website you are visiting is letting all its friends put sticky notes on your back. For the simple reason that it benefits from it. Sometimes the website is paid in information: the parties collecting the data can give it lots of useful statistics about the demographics and personal characteristics of its visitors. But more often the website you are visiting wants to be able to advertise to you in the future after you leave the site. And access to the third party's vast trove of tracking data allows it to do just that (for a price, of course).

You might wonder who the parties are that trail you around the Internet. Some are household names like Google and Yahoo; others are newcomers like Rocket Fuel, which Mark Torrance estimates has placed cookies on about 90 percent of all personal computers in the United States. To see why these cookies are so valuable, you need to understand the power of cross-referenced information. Simple facts, useless by themselves, can become very precious when combined. Together, these facts can be used to assign you to what's called an "affinity group" that indicates your preferences or likelihood to buy a particular product.

For instance, if you read vegetarian recipes online, you may be much more likely than the average person to be interested in trying out a new yoga studio in your neighborhood. The chance that someone random will click on an ad for a golf vacation may be one in ten thousand, but if you are male, it may increase to one in a thousand, and if you've looked up who won the Masters Tournament, it may rise to one in a hundred. If you watch the entire *Twilight* movie trilogy, you may be inclined to purchase its soundtrack, but if you also watched *Cosmopolis* and *Bel Ami,* you may be likely to buy a magazine featuring an interview with Robert Pattinson (who starred in all these movies).

Or, most important, if you recently visited a web page for a specific product but didn't buy it, say, a certain model of running shoes, you are far more likely to respond to an ad for that product if it is shown to you in the near future. The problem is that once you have left their website, the makers of those running shoes have no way to communicate with you again. So that's where the parties depositing the cookies on your computer come in. When you turn up somewhere else, for instance, on a website to make a dinner reservation, they recognize you as the same person who looked at the shoes last week, and can show you an ad reminding you of your interest. This, called "retargeting," is one of the most valuable forms of online advertising today.

Companies like Rocket Fuel have built elaborate mathematical models to predict how likely you are to respond to a particular ad from one of the advertisers that they represent. And they know, statistically speaking, just how much you are worth to each of those advertisers. So they know how much the advertiser can afford to pay to put a specific ad in front of you when you load a page.

And that's where synthetic intellects come in. Keeping this analysis up to date is a task of monumental complexity far exceeding human capabilities. To do this well, they must collect and analyze a staggeringly large amount of data on a continuing basis. But machine learning systems with access to enormous computing power and data storage are equal to the task. They are perpetually sifting through this river of information, panning it for gold in the form of valuable correlations and waiting to jump into the fray when you next visit a page, regardless of where that page happens to be.

The problem is that the synthetic intellects of all the other parties that have cookies on your computer are doing the same thing. Each of them represents a differing collection of advertisers, and each predicts different values for showing you different ads on different parts of different pages with different browsers at different times of day.

Now let's turn this around and look at it from the perspective of someone who simply wants to operate his or her own website and make money by selling advertising. Selling ad space to each individual advertiser is entirely impractical, except for a handful of the largest and most successful websites. Even selling the space to intermediaries (like Rocket Fuel) that represent multiple advertisers would be a nightmare. So elaborate electronic ad exchanges have sprung up to perform an actual price auction for each ad that quietly appears on the pages you load. The operators of websites simply consign their available inventory of ad space to the ad exchange. The intermediaries also sign up, and the games begin.

When you load a page, and it calls for a specific size of ad, this information is transmitted to the ad exchange. It is immediately put out for bid to the intermediaries, who look to see if they have a cookie on your computer. If so, they perform an elaborate evaluation to estimate how much they want to pay for that opportunity, taking into account every time they have ever seen you, where you have been, and what you have done in the past. They also consider which website you are currently visiting, what content is on the page you are viewing, and how likely you are to do business with the advertisers available in their portfolio.

Now things get complicated. The intermediaries might also purchase information about you from other companies that aren't in the advertising placement business but have agreed to share cookies with them for a fee. Even at the lightning speed of the Internet, it isn't practical to perform multiple auction rounds. So each bidder selects a particular ad from its roster and makes a single best offer. It also tells the ad exchange which advertiser's message it plans to display, because the websites serving the ads don't want just anything to appear on their pages. (For instance, a site catering to children may refuse ads for certain products targeted to adults, such as promoting casinos, even though the person viewing the page may be a good prospect for such. Or a diabetes information site may not want to show ads for sweets.) But nearly all sites refuse to show ads from their competitors. Finally, the ad exchange awards the opportunity to the highest bidder but charges it only the price of the second-highest bidder (which encourages participants to place their best, highest bid).

So, after quite probably expending more computing power than was used to put the first man on the moon, an ad seamlessly appears on the page you are loading . . . offering special vitamins for your cat to help fight feline leukemia. Amazing—how did they know that you just got a cat? Yikes, if they figured that out, what if they're right about the leukemia too?

During a recent conversation, Rocket Fuel's CEO, George John, pointed out to me the irony that the art of persuasion, something you might reasonably regard as a uniquely human endeavor, is better done by synthetic intellects. Numerous customer testimonials on the Rocket Fuel website remark how much better Rocket Fuel is at spending their ad budget than they could possibly be themselves.

You may notice that I've glossed over one important question: how do the bidders know what showing a particular ad is really worth to the advertiser? The answer is that an equally sophisticated and entirely parallel system exists for the advertisers to provide feedback to the intermediaries when you take an action that relates to an ad they showed you. That action might be clicking on the ad immediately, or it might be independently visiting that advertiser's website in the future. (This delayed behavior is called "viewthrough attribution.")

Toward the end of my visit, Mark Torrance demonstrated the

remarkable precision with which his computers can predict and influence your behavior by showing me how he estimates the likelihood that you will buy a pizza from one of his clients (a major international fast-food pizza franchise) within two weeks after you see one of their ads. Selecting a green cell off an elaborately colored chart called a "heat map," I could see that for a carefully selected group of consumers, between 9.125 and 11.345 percent of them would order a pizza from his client within two weeks, *even without his client knowing whether they ever ate pizza at all.* The actual figure, as later reported back to him by the client, was 10.9 percent.

The various participants in this arduous process aren't exactly friends, and so all sorts of shenanigans and game playing ensue. For instance, because the winning bidder in any auction knows what price the runner-up bid, it can infer a lot about who else is out there gunning for the same inventory and what those other parties are willing to pay. So the bidding parties engage in complex strategies to outwit the other participants, like professional poker players sizing each other up by intentionally losing hands. And the ad exchanges' synthetic intellects, which manage all the bidding, hardly behave as angels. They study each bidder's strategies and increase their own profits by cherry-picking opportunities or pitting similar bidders against each other to run up the price.

With so much energy invested in this process, you might expect that these ads would be quite precious, but the opposite is true. Despite the Herculean effort these synthetic intellects put into each and every battle, the right to serve an ad through one of these ad exchanges might sell for as little as $0.00005, or five ten-thousandths of a penny. (In advertising terminology, this is a five-cent CPM—cost per thousand.) But, as the saying goes, they make it up on volume.

Three friends founded Rocket Fuel in 2008 and, as of this writing, the company is worth approximately $2 billion. As you might suspect, both Mark Torrance and CEO George John studied artificial intelligence at Stanford.

So what's the root cause of all this electronic pandemonium— computer programs fighting each other over the opportunity to game our financial systems or influence our consumer behavior? Can't synthetic intellects just play nice, like decent civilized people?

The answer is surprisingly simple. These systems are designed to achieve singular goals, without awareness of or concern for any side effects. As I will explain in later chapters, there's no incentive for combatants in these new electronic coliseums to show any mercy to each other, or to pay anything more than the bare minimum they must to get what they want. Similarly, they will charge the most they possibly can in order to extract the maximum profit possible.

As synthetic intellects increasingly encroach on areas previously the exclusive domain of humans, oblivious to the broader social context, they are prone to behaving in ways that society would find repugnant. Stealing a parking place that someone else is patiently waiting for; buying all the batteries on a Home Depot shelf before a big storm, leaving none for anyone else; perhaps blocking a wheelchair from using the curb ramp while waiting for the light to change.

But as these systems become ever more capable and autonomous, the danger grows dramatically. For instance, imagine a future in which someone buys the latest model of general-purpose robotic personal assistant and instructs it to apply its immense abilities toward becoming the world's most successful chess player. The human may have in mind that the robot will study the games of grand masters, practice against other players, and enter various competitions. But without guidance, the robot may instead formulate more reliable strategies, such as threatening the families of credible competitors in the hope of throwing them off their game, sabotaging planes carrying better players to the contests, or otherwise incapacitating anyone who might interfere with its ability to meet its assigned goal.[4]

And what, if anything, should we do about the potential dangers posed by synthetic intellects? The answer is more nuanced. We need to control when and where synthetic intellects (or any electronic agent, for that matter) are permitted to act on our behalf. This need is particularly acute when they commingle with human agents.

I'll start with this latter issue. We frequently rely on a hidden assumption of a level playing field to allocate resources in a reasonable way. When Ticketmaster first went online, it greatly increased the convenience of getting a ticket to a concert. (I'm old enough to remember having to drive to the nearest Tower Records for this purpose, where Ticketmaster located its specialized high-tech terminals. Actually, I'm old enough to remember the bad old days *before* Ticketmaster, when you simply went to the concert to stand in line and took your chances.) But soon after Ticketmaster was available on the Internet, scalpers began using programs to scarf up online concert tickets the moment they became available. Lacking a regulatory framework to address the problem, Ticketmaster has attempted technological fixes, such as requiring you to interpret those annoying little brain twisters known as CAPTCHAs, to little effect, because the scalpers simply employ armies of live humans, mostly in third world countries, to decode them.[5]

The problem here has nothing to do with whether you use an agent to purchase a ticket. It's fine for you to buy a ticket on behalf of a friend or to pay someone else to do it. The issue arises when we permit electronic agents to compete for resources with human agents. In most circumstances, it violates our intuitive sense of fairness. That's why there are separate tournaments for human and computer chess players. It's also why allowing programs to trade securities alongside humans is problematic, though I think we would have a hard time putting that genie back in the bottle.

Lines and queues are great cultural equalizers because they force everyone to incur the cost of waiting, spending his or her own personal time. That's why it somehow seems wrong when lobbyists pay people to stand in line for them at congressional hearings, squeezing ordinary citizens out of their chance to attend. Some argue that waiting in line extracts a higher price from the wealthy than the less fortunate, but that misses the point: there are some resources we don't want to be economically fungible. It's the reason it's illegal to buy or sell votes, or kidneys, in most civilized countries.

This same principle, appropriately generalized, can apply to just about any circumstance where electronic agents compete with humans—not just to lines. Do the participants differ in their ability, or the cost they pay, to access the resource? This question needs to be answered on a case-by-case basis, but the concept is clear. For instance, suppose I send my robot to move my car every two hours to avoid a parking ticket, or instruct my self-driving car to repark itself. Will we judge that cost sufficiently equivalent to doing it myself to consider it fair to those without a robotic driver or car to spare? What if it costs me as much to send the robot as it would for you to send your human administrative assistant?

I contend that the brawl for the right to display an ad to you seems a lot fairer than having HFT programs participate in the securities markets. That's because, in the case of ads, humans don't typically participate in the placements (though they did in the early days of the Internet), so every bidder is on a more equal footing.

Once again, our biological baggage works against our interests. It's easy to physically see if the boss's robot is moving his or her car. It's a lot harder to tell if someone has written a clever program to reserve an entire row of camping spots at Yellowstone Park the weekend you want to go the moment the sites are released to the public—while you're still loading the web page. We need to incorporate these concepts into our public discussion so we can extend our sense of fairness into the electronic domain. Right now, it's an untamed territory shrouded in perpetual darkness that invites all manner of skullduggery.

But there are much more subtle problems with the use of synthetic intellects as agents.

**5.** Officer, Arrest That Robot

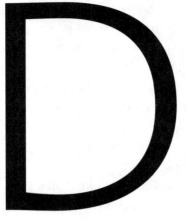uring the Middle Ages, animals could be tried for criminal offenses. There are documented stories of cases brought against chickens, rats, field mice, bees, gnats, and pigs.[1] Back then, people apparently thought animals capable of knowing right from wrong and behaving accordingly, in a way that we don't today. They believed that animals had what's called *moral agency.*

A widely accepted characterization of moral agents is that they must be capable of two things. They must be able to perceive the morally pertinent consequences of their actions, and they must be able to choose between the relevant courses of action.

Curiously, neither of these two requirements relies on any subjective, innate sense of right or wrong. It simply says that agents have to be able to control their own actions and evaluate the effects of their actions against some putative moral standard. Whether that standard is self-generated, whether they understand the theory underlying that standard, whether they agree with it or not, whether they can "feel" the difference between righteousness and sin—all that is irrelevant.

Consider the predicament of the psychopath. He or she has little or no ability to feel empathy or remorse for his or her actions. However, many if not most psychopaths are quite intelligent, certainly capable of both understanding moral concepts and controlling their own behavior accordingly—they just don't experience an emotional reaction to moral questions. Psychologists estimate that over 1 percent of the U.S. population are psychopaths.[2] And yet, we don't see one out of a hundred people running around committing crimes willy-nilly. Psychopaths may privately wonder what the big deal is, but they understand how they are supposed to behave, and most somehow manage to suck it up and get along with the rest of us.

Today we may find the medieval notion that animals can commit crimes laughable, but the modern interpretation of moral agency is hardly confined to humans.

In 2010, the oil rig Deepwater Horizon in the Gulf of Mexico suffered an underwater blowout. Eleven workers were killed, and large quantities of oil fouled the water and beaches. The federal government filed *criminal*—in addition to civil—charges against BP, the oil company that owned the rig. The company settled the charges for $4 billion. That's on top of large civil penalties and fines.

The criminal case against BP illustrates that you don't need to be conscious or sentient to have moral agency. In our legal system, a corporation is considered to have moral agency and can be held criminally liable. That is, BP was supposed to know better and be capable of doing the right things to ensure the accident didn't happen, but in this case, it failed to do so. The corporation itself, as distinct from its employees, had a duty to put sufficient controls in place to avoid incidents like this one.

So modern legal theory accepts the notion that both people and corporations can be moral agents, and therefore can be charged with crimes. How about a synthetic intellect? Can it meet the requirements for moral responsibility as well?

Yes, it can. If it is sufficiently capable of sensing the morally relevant aspects of its environment, and it has a choice of actions, it qualifies as a moral agent. These systems don't have to be very sophisticated to cross this seemingly anthropological boundary. A robotic lawnmower may be able to see that it's about to run over a child's leg, as opposed to a stick, and it may be capable of selecting whether to stop or continue. The question, of course, is how it is supposed to "know" it should stop in one case but should proceed in the other. Without some sort of guidance, we wouldn't expect it, a priori, to make a good decision.

This problem is far from theoretical. An active intellectual debate is quietly taking place sub rosa regarding how to program autonomous vehicles. It's easy to construct ethically challenging scenarios for such products that are virtually certain to occur, no matter how much we try to avoid them. Your self-driving car can run over a dog to save your life: pretty clear what you would want it to do. But what if it has to choose between running over an elderly couple or a bunch of kids crossing the street? How about a Sophie's Choice of which of your own children to kill, the one in the front seat or the one in the back? We can ignore such questions because they are so painful to consider, but that itself would be an immoral act.

Okay, so we'll grit our teeth and program in a moral code. Sounds like an engineering problem, but it's not that simple. Despite considerable attention to this topic, there's no accepted consensus among experts as to what such a moral code might look like. Over the centuries, philosophers have developed a rich panoply of ethical theories, and arguments over which is best—or even viable— that continue unabated to this day.

Even if we could reach some consensus on this difficult question, there's no reason to believe that the result could easily be reduced to practice and implemented programmatically. Some researchers in the emerging field of computational ethics, which seeks to create "artificial moral agents," have tried using a "top-down" approach. They select and implement moral principles a priori, then build systems that attempt to respect those principles (duty-based normative ethics). Others pursue a "bottom-up" strategy, relying on machine learning algorithms presented with a large collection of relevant examples. But this approach has a significant drawback. Like humans, machines are far from guaranteed to acquire and implement acceptable moral principles, much less be able to articulate them. Other approaches include "case-based reasoning," essentially, resolving moral challenges by relating them to a catalog of (hopefully similar) known cases. One challenge dogging this nascent field is that at least some of our own moral sense seems to be rooted in our human ability to feel sympathy and compassion—we instinctively reason that if something hurts us, it's probably not right for us to inflict it on others. This shortcut to ethical behavior is presumably unavailable to machines. In short, we're a long way from developing a curriculum to teach engineers the practice of moral programming.[3]

Quite aside from the issue of machine moral agency is the question of who is responsible when it makes a bad decision. To answer this, it's useful to understand the legal theory behind the relationship between "principals" and their "agents." To explore this, let's return to the BP case.

You might wonder how a corporation can commit a criminal act, as opposed to its employees committing criminal acts. Eleven people died on the Deepwater Horizon, but that doesn't mean that any particular individual was negligent or engaged in criminal activity. On the contrary, every employee may simply have carried out his or her assigned duties, and none of those duties were to kill eleven people.

The employees were the *means* by which the corporation committed the crime. By the same theory, when you hold up a bank, your legs are the *means* by which you walk into the bank. Your legs, of course, aren't criminally liable. But there's a big difference between a means of getting something done, like your legs carrying you into the bank, and the managers on the Deepwater Horizon failing to detect or correct a potentially dangerous situation. The managers are considered to be "agents" of the corporation, and so potentially shoulder some of the liability.

An agent is an independent party who is authorized, by mutual agreement, to act on behalf of a principal. Now your legs are neither an independent party nor are they in a position to knowingly enter into a mutual agreement to act on your behalf. On the other hand, an employee of BP is an independent party who can knowingly act on BP's behalf.

When acting on your behalf, your agent has what's called a fiduciary responsibility to carry out your intent and protect your interests—but only within certain limits. For instance, if your agent knowingly commits a crime on your behalf, that doesn't get him or her off the hook. If I hire you to kill my romantic rival, you share responsibility for the murder because you are presumed to understand that you are part of a conspiracy to break the law.

But what if an agent commits a crime and doesn't know he or she is doing it? I say, "Here, press this button," you comply, and a bomb goes off at the Super Bowl. You acted as my agent, but you are responsible only if you reasonably should have known the consequences.

Now let's turn this around. Suppose the agent commits a crime in the service of a principal without the principal's knowledge. I tell you to go get me $100 from the bank. You go down to the bank with a gun and hand the teller a note ordering him or her to put the money in unmarked bills into a paper bag. You return and give me the bag. Am I responsible for your theft? Under most circumstances, the answer is no. (I'm oversimplifying a bit, because if the supposedly innocent party benefited from the crime, they can also be held legally responsible even if they were unaware of it.)

There's a long history of legal principles and precedents addressing who is responsible for what in a principal-agency relationship—or, more accurately, apportioning liability between the parties when their relative responsibility is unclear.

In the BP case, the government concluded that the actions of the individual employees didn't themselves constitute criminal acts, but these acts taken in aggregate did. So it indicted BP itself, as a principal with sufficiently broad responsibilities.

So modern legal theory accepts the notion that both people and corporations can be principals and agents, and can independently be charged with crimes. How about an intelligent machine? Who is responsible when a synthetic intellect acts on your behalf? You might think the obvious answer is you, and today that's probably right. But this isn't entirely fair, and it's likely to change in the future, for good reasons.

Consider the following scenario. Imagine that you purchase a personal home robot that is capable of taking the elevator down from your tenth-floor Greenwich Village apartment, crossing the street, and purchasing a caramel flan Frappuccino for you from Starbucks. (This isn't entirely science fiction. A prototype of just such a robot was recently demonstrated at Stanford.)[4] In addition to being preprogrammed with a variety of general behavioral principles, the robot is able to hone its navigational and social skills by watching the behavior of the people it encounters. After all, customs and practices vary from place to place. It might be appropriate to shake hands with females you meet in New York, but it is forbidden in Iran unless you are related. Unbeknownst to you, your robot recently witnessed a rare event, a Good Samaritan subduing a purse snatcher until the police arrived, earning the approval and admiration of a burgeoning crowd of spectators.

On the way to fetch your coffee, your robot witnesses a man grappling with a woman, then taking her purse, over her apparent objections. It infers that a crime is taking place and, consistent with its general programming and its specific experience, it wrestles the man to the ground and detains him while calling 911.

When the police arrive, the man explains that he and his wife were merely having an animated tussle over the car keys to determine who was going to drive. His wife confirms the story. Oops! They turn their attention to your well-intentioned but hapless robot, which dutifully explains that it was merely acting on your instructions to fetch a drink. Incensed, the two insist that the police arrest you for assault.

Your defense attorney's argument is simple: you didn't do it, the robot did. You purchased the robot in good-faith reliance on its design and were using it in accordance with its intended purpose, so the company that sold you the robot should be held responsible for the incident.

But that company also has lawyers, and they successfully argue that they have met all reasonable standards of product liability and acted with due diligence and care. They point out that in millions of hours of use, this is the first event of its kind. From their perspective, this was simply a regrettable though unpredictable freak accident no different from an autonomous vehicle driving into a sinkhole that suddenly appears.

Perplexed at this liability gap, the judge looks for precedents. He finds one in the antebellum "Slave Codes" (as they were called) of the seventeenth and eighteenth centuries.[5] Prior to the Civil War, various states and jurisdictions maintained a separate (and very unequal) body of laws to govern the treatment, legal status, and responsibilities of slaves. For the most part, these codes characterized slaves as property having limited rights and protections, particularly from their owners. While we certainly believe today that southern plantation slaves were conscious human beings, deserving of the same basic human rights as all others, it's worth noting that not everyone at that time agreed with this assessment.[6] Regardless, these codes inevitably held the slaves, not the owners, legally culpable for their crimes and subjected them to punishment.

The judge in this case sees a parallel between the status of a slave—who is legal "property" but is also capable of making his or her own independent decisions—and your robot. He decides that the appropriate punishment in this case is that the robot's memory will be erased, to expunge its purse-snatching experience, and, as reparation for the crime, the robot will be consigned to the injured party's custody for a period of twelve months.[7]

The victim of the crime feels this is an acceptable resolution and will be happy to have a free, obedient servant for the next year. You are unhappy that you will temporarily lose the use of your robot and then have to retrain it, but it beats going to prison for assault.

And thus begins a new trail of precedents and body of law.

To recap, there's no requirement in our laws that a moral agent be human or conscious, as the BP Deepwater Horizon case demonstrates. The relevant entity must merely be capable of recognizing the moral consequences of its actions and be able to act independently. Recall that synthetic intellects are commonly equipped with machine learning programs that develop unique internal representations based on the examples in the training set. I use this pile of jargon to avoid the danger inherent in using anthropomorphic language, but only because we don't yet have the common words to describe these concepts any other way. Otherwise, I would simply say that synthetic intellects think and act based on their own experience, which in this case your robot clearly did. It just happened to be wrong. It may have been acting as your legal agent, but since you didn't know what it was doing, even as its principal you aren't responsible—it is.

There's only one problem. If you accept that a synthetic intellect can commit a crime, how on earth do you discipline it? The judge in this case effectively punished the robot's owner and compensated the victim, but did he mete out justice to the robot?

For guidance, consider how corporations are treated. Obviously, you can't punish a corporation the same way you can a human. You can't sentence a corporation to ten years in prison or take away its right to vote. In the words of Edward Thurlow, lord chancellor of England at the turn of the nineteenth century, "Did you ever expect a corporation to have a conscience, when it has no soul to be damned, and no body to be kicked?"[8]

The key here is that humans, corporations, and synthetic intellects all have one thing in common: a purpose or goal. (At least within the context of the crime.) A human may commit a crime for a variety of reasons, such as for material gain, to stay out of prison (paradoxically), or to eliminate a romantic competitor. And the punishments we mete out relate to those goals. We may deprive the perpetrator of life (capital punishment), liberty (incarceration), or the ability to pursue happiness (a restraining order, for instance).

When corporations commit crimes, we don't lock them away. Instead, we levy fines. Because the goal of a corporation is to make money, at least most of the time, this is a significant deterrent to bad behavior. We can also void contracts, exclude it from markets, or make its actions subject to external oversight, as is sometimes the case in antitrust litigation. In the extreme, we can deprive it of life (that is, close it down).

So we've already accepted the concept that not all perpetrators should suffer the same consequences. Not only should the punishment fit the crime, the punishment should fit the criminal. Punishing a synthetic intellect requires interfering with its ability to achieve its goals. This may not have an emotional impact as it might on a human, but it does serve important purposes of our legal system—deterrence and rehabilitation. A synthetic intellect, rationally programmed to pursue its goals, will alter its behavior to achieve its objectives when it encounters obstacles. This may be as simple as seeing examples of other instances of itself held to account for mistakes.

Note that, in contrast to most mass-produced artifacts, instances of synthetic intellects need not be equivalent, for the same reason that identical twins are not the same person. Each may learn from its own unique experiences and draw its own idiosyncratic conclusions, as our fictional robot did in the assault case.

For a more contemporary example, consider a credit card fraud detection program that uses machine learning algorithms. It may inadvertently run afoul of antidiscrimination laws by taking the race of the cardholder into account, or it may have independently discovered some other variable that is closely correlated with race. Unscrambling the digital omelet in which this knowledge is embedded may be entirely impractical, so the penalty might be to delete the entire database.

That may sound innocuous, but it's not. It could have substantial economic consequences for the bank or owner of that program, which has relied on billions of real-time transactions collected over many years to fine-tune its performance. You can bet the owner would fight hard to avoid this outcome.

But forced amnesia is not the only way to interfere with a synthetic intellect's goals. It may be possible to revoke its authority to act. In fact, the licensing of synthetic intellects to permit their use and holding them responsible for their own behavior go hand in hand.

For instance, it's likely that the government or insurance companies will review and approve each model of autonomous vehicle, pretty much as they do for all vehicles now. The same is true for computer programs that operate medical equipment, which fall under the definition of medical devices. In the future, we may revoke authority by recalling the medallion of an autonomous taxi, requiring a legal program to retake the bar exam, or deleting the account credentials from an automated trading program.

So synthetic intellects will be accorded rights (for example, in the form of licenses) and will have responsibilities (for example, to refrain from damaging the property of others), just like other entities that can sense, act, and make choices. The legal framework for this is called *personhood.*

Late-night comedians delight in making fun of the well-established legal principle that corporations are people, for instance, in the aftermath of *Citizens United v. Federal Election Commission* (2010), in which the U.S. Supreme Court affirmed that corporations are entitled to the free-speech protection of the First Amendment to the Constitution. Of course, this doesn't mean what the comedians pretend it means, that judges foolishly equate corporations with humans. It merely means that corporations have selected rights and responsibilities, and the legal shorthand for this is personhood.[9]

The functional parallels between corporations and synthetic intellects are so strong that courts will likely establish the principle that synthetic intellects can be *artificial persons* in an attempt to make sense of a patchwork of precedents like the robotic assault case described earlier. The attendant rights and responsibilities will evolve over time.

The most important of these are the right to enter into contracts and own assets. Arguably, we already permit computer-based systems to enter into contracts when they trade stocks, or when you make an online purchase. It's just that their owners are the legal entities bound by those contracts.

There will also be strong pressure to permit artificial persons to own assets because such assets can be subject to seizure or fines independent of the artificial person's owners. In the robotic assault example, the judge effectively condemned the robot to a year of servitude precisely because its own labor was the only asset it had. There was no way to order the robot to pay a fine, and presumably the judge thought this sentence better than asking the owner to pay. But if the robot had its own burgeoning bank account, it would be a very tempting target.

Owners of synthetic intellects will also favor granting contractual and property rights to artificial persons because this will have the side effect of insulating their own assets from liability—the most common motivation for forming a corporation today.

Unlike most predictions, this isn't fanciful speculation about one possible future among many. On the contrary, it will be hard to prevent, because the effect can be simulated today by wrapping each synthetic intellect in its own legal corporation, just as your lawyer or doctor might be a "professional corporation" or LLC. If I were the owner and operator of a fleet of autonomous taxis, I would seriously consider incorporating each vehicle as an asset of its own legal entity for precisely this reason; I wouldn't want a single catastrophic mistake to bankrupt my entire enterprise. Other than that, I would leave my roving minions to mint money as best they could, squirreling away their profits for me to collect like honey from a beehive.

Which leads us back to the essential problem with intelligent machines as agents. They will ruthlessly pursue the goals we assign them, outcompeting humans, and may be under our control only nominally—at least until we develop the ethical and legal framework for integrating them as productive partners into human society. As they enrich our lives, enhance our prosperity, and increase our leisure, the irresistible and undeniable benefits of all this technology will obscure a disquieting truth: synthetic intellects and forged laborers will be running around as independent agents, performing work and making money on behalf of their owners, without regard to the consequences to others or to society in general. Instead, as in the case of the HFT programs, they are likely to be skimming off the lion's share of the enormous wealth they create for the benefit of a few lucky individuals.

As you might expect, this scenario has already started. Super-human omniscient systems observe our individual and group behavior, then guide us to what we purchase, listen to, watch, and read—while the profits quietly pile up elsewhere. You don't have to look very far to find an example of how this affects you—there's no waiting on checkout 1 in the Amazon cloud!

# 6. America, Land of the Free Shipping

first met Jeff Bezos at a 1996 retreat for CEOs of the venture capital firm of Kleiner, Perkins, Caufield and Byers. This may sound like a Davos- or Bohemian Club–style conclave of movers and shakers, but nothing could be farther from the truth. Most of the thirty or so attendees were relative newcomers to the Silicon Valley scene. Jeff was one of the first to realize that the opening of the Internet to commercial use might create significant business opportunities. Prior to that, it was restricted to government and research institutions for official business, and access was controlled by the Defense Advanced Projects Agency (DARPA).

With a bachelor's degree in electrical engineering and computer science, and a series of technical jobs on Wall Street under his belt, Jeff had landed a position with a secretive but highly successful investment firm founded by an affable Columbia professor ten years his senior—Dave Shaw. Yes, the same Dave Shaw who pioneered programmed trading, founded D. E. Shaw and Company, and earned the Wall Street nickname King Quant. But one day, for reasons only he and Dave know, Jeff quit to seek his fortunes elsewhere. He and his new wife piled their possessions in their car and took off for Seattle. During the ride, he worked on a business plan while, I must assume, his wife drove.

Jeff was a high-energy, first-time entrepreneur with a boisterous laugh and a quirky smile. It seemed to me, as a fellow CEO of an early Internet startup, that Jeff exhibited an astounding lack of caution. I was always amazed that he would make multimillion-dollar business commitments with complete confidence that, when the time came, he would be able to raise the money required. And he was always right. Jeff's idea was to start an online bookstore, which he gave the odd name of Amazon. As I recall, when we met, he was struggling with the minor problem that Amazon was too small to warrant the attention of book publishers, not to mention that he had no way to buy or sell books. We were both trying to figure out how to take payments over the Internet as, at the time, no respectable bank would process credit card transactions transmitted over some sort of public computer network they had never heard of. If you didn't see or talk to your customers, how could you know they were who they claimed to be?

Lacking the capital and the connections to invest in ware-houses and inventory, Jeff did the next best thing: he made a deal with the largest wholesaler at the time, Ingram Book Group. In-gram stocked and shipped books in small quantities to independ-ent bookstores around the country, and the wholesaler also served as a resource for major chains if they ran short of stock locally and needed a quick delivery. The advantage, from Jeff's perspective, was that Ingram would drop-ship orders as small as a single book, though I suspect the company wasn't very happy about it.

My startup idea was that goods didn't have to be sold online at fixed prices. So along with two partners I started Onsale.com, the first auction site on the Internet.[1] But Jeff learned an important les-son from Dave Shaw that I had missed, at least at first: *the real value wasn't in the inventory, it was in the data.*

Jeff recognized that the same basic principles that D. E. Shaw and Company applied to securities transactions could be applied to information provided by *people*. For him, at least initially, the fact that he was dealing with physical products was incidental, or at least secondary; the inventory and logistics were matters that could be subcontracted to third parties for a fee. The real essence of his business was the accumulating book reviews and purchasing histories of his customers. He recognized that the time it took to read a book represented a higher cost for most buyers than the nominal price of the product. Time spent digging into a read you didn't like was wasted. So why not let his customers curate his products the way an experienced bricks-and-mortar bookstore salesperson might do? He correctly guessed that the opportunity to pontificate publicly and help others was reward enough for their efforts.

Stating the obvious, Amazon has not only revolutionized virtually all aspects of the book industry—with the possible exception of the writing—it has also grown to become one of the world's largest sellers of just about everything. But there's another way to look at Amazon's remarkable rise.

When we describe Amazon as an "online retailer," we think of it as a digital analog of a physical store. But there's an alternative way to describe Amazon: as an application and expansion of D. E. Shaw and Company's securities-trading strategies to the buying and selling of retail goods.

When Amazon was processing your order by transmitting it to Ingram for delivery, it was engaging in the same sort of arbitrage as Dave Shaw's supercomputers: two simultaneous transactions that were guaranteed to make a profit, as long as they both settled. The first transaction was with you—an agreement to sell you a book at a particular price and deliver it within a mutually agreeable time frame (otherwise known as a futures contract), and a separate transaction was with Ingram to purchase a book for delivery to a specified destination. By constantly adjusting its "ask" price to you, Amazon locked in a known price spread as its gross profit. And like the programmed trading algorithm, the whole scheme worked because Amazon had better information than you did. Specifically, it knew where and how to purchase the item at a better price (that is, at Ingram), something you were not privy to nor could take advantage of directly.[2]

Jeff understands now, as he did then, that the power was in the data. He's spent nearly two decades amassing an unprecedented array of statistics about individual and collective purchasing habits, including detailed personal information on more than 200 million active buyers. He mainly did this by losing money, but that's sure to stop once your continued patronage is statistically assured, the potential pool of new buyers starts to shrink, and Jeff decides to curtail his investment and expansion efforts. (In business terminology, when the cost of new customer acquisition converges with the customers' lifetime value.) As with other monopolies, once suppliers have no choice but to deal with Amazon, which is certainly true for the book industry, and customers are as loyal as courtesans, there's a myriad of ways to extract the premium attendant to market dominance. (Contrary to popular belief, monopolies are not illegal. It's how they use their market power to restrict competition that sometimes causes them to run afoul of the law.)

But how does Amazon put this cornucopia of information to productive use? For starters, by adjusting prices on the fly to achieve certain business objectives. As long as investors are willing to permit the company the leeway to grow at the expense of profits, Amazon wants to build your confidence that when you buy from them, you are getting the best, or at least a very good, price. The easiest way to meet this objective is to actually do it. So the company constantly monitors competitive prices, and adjusts its own prices accordingly.

If you're an Amazon regular, you'll notice that the prices of items in your shopping cart inexplicably change over time, sometimes by trivial amounts. Whole businesses have sprung up to monitor these fluctuations to help you snag the best price.[3] The question is why. The seemingly random character of these changes suggests that they are the result of an automated process, most likely website crawlers pulling prices from other sites, or even on Amazon itself, for, in addition to selling directly, Amazon is a marketplace where others can sell the same goods. A price study at the University of Michigan in the summer of 2000 found that the price of a DVD on Amazon varied by up to 20 percent depending on the user's browser and account. When a group of customers accused Amazon of charging them different prices for the same items, the company attributed the discrepancies to "a very brief test to see how customers respond to various prices."[4]

Most people think it's illegal for companies to charge different prices to different customers, but there's nothing illegal or inappropriate about such practices as long as certain criteria—such as race, gender, and sexual orientation—are not used to discriminate. Amazon is not unique in this regard. A 2005 University of Pennsylvania research report discusses how grocery store loyalty card programs offer differently valued discount coupons at checkout depending on such factors as how brand-loyal you appear to be.[5] In other words, if you were inclined to buy the item anyway, why almost literally give away the store?

The problem here is that all this wonderful laissez-faire is a prelude to *à prendre ou à laisser*—take it or leave it.[6] The free flow of information around the Internet creates winner-take-all markets, and online retailing is no exception.[7]

Before the Internet, there were two points of friction that enabled a retailing market vigorous enough to profitably accommodate multiple sellers of identical goods. The first was information. How much more difficult was it to comparison shop, when you had to drive to a competitor's store or search for their ads in the local newspaper, hoping to find the same item?

The other point of friction for retail goods used to be the effective cost of delivery. So what if the lamp you want to buy is available for less at a store one hundred miles away—it's not worth the drive. In principle this could also be a problem on the Internet, because the cost to ship an item from a warehouse in New Jersey to New York City should be less than the cost to ship the same item to San Francisco. But Amazon has solved that problem as well, by using its economies of scale to pre-position the goods locally near major population centers, a luxury unavailable to most current or potential future competitors.

These two friction points are closely related, and Amazon has conflated them to brilliant advantage. Separating the cost to you into a product price and a shipping price is a fiction subject to manipulation. Mincing the total price into components is a time-honored way of obscuring true costs, though in the end it all boils down to one total figure.

Examples of this technique in other fields are the "destination," "delivery," and "documentation" fees added to the sticker price of cars. Medical billing has raised this art of confounding consumers to a new level of absurdity, sending facility (hospital) charges and doctor bills separately with different due dates, so you rarely know how much a service is costing you at the time you actually pay.[8] Even online, trying to compare the features and prices of different models of computers is virtually impossible even for experts, as you need to determine precisely what is included and what you will need to purchase separately. In this regard, Apple Computer is a model of consumer transparency.

Like the medical care industry, Amazon pioneered a new way to obscure the price you pay not only by separating the required information into two disparate parts but by literally making it impossible to discern your total cost until long after you have actually made a purchase. The innovation was to charge you a fixed annual shipping fee—Amazon Prime–regardless of how many purchases you have made or will make during that year. (Arguably, Amazon Prime is an updated variant of the buying-club strategy of charging an annual membership fee.) This conjures the oxymoronic illusion of free shipping that you pay for. Paraphrasing economist Milton Friedman, there's no such thing as free shipping—someone always pays. Is this fee worth it to you? Would you be better off paying a higher price that includes delivery from an alternative vendor? Only Amazon knows for sure.

Persuading you to prepay for shipping not only discourages you from shopping elsewhere, it makes rational buying impossible. This is at least one motivation for Amazon's commendable focus on customer satisfaction; as long as you're happy with the company, there's little reason to question its pricing practices or to comparison shop—even if you could.

But the company has taken the doctrine of information asymmetry one step further. Amazon's network of warehouses is so extensive, it has adopted the remarkable policy of permitting its competitors to list their own products on Amazon's website and use Amazon's own facilities for fulfillment. You might think this is an egalitarian act that serves to level the playing field by giving the "little guy" access to the same advantages that Amazon enjoys. But in reality, this ingenious tactic gives Amazon two additional potential competitive advantages: it has a picture window into competitors' sales and prices, and ultimately the strategy gives Amazon control over its competitors' costs because it can adjust the rates it charges for these services. After all, no one said it had to charge competitors only their proportional share of the fulfillment costs. Want to take over the market for electric toothbrushes? No problem, charge your competitors more to stock and ship their inventory than it costs you to handle the same products.

The common thread behind these business tactics is to acquire an enduring information advantage over customers and competitors, deftly wrapped in a narrative of low prices, outstanding service, and fair play.

I think Amazon is an amazing company and Jeff Bezos is a great guy, but there's another reason the financial markets value the company at more than six hundred times earnings (2013), when the average is around twenty times earnings: they look forward to the inevitable time when the company extracts monopoly prices after locking in its customers and scorching the earth of competitors. And this is as it should be. Shoppers aren't stupid; they will go where they get the best all-around deal, including convenience, service, and other factors. They aren't concerned with whether their short-term purchasing behavior may restructure the retailing landscape to the detriment of future consumers any more than the original residents of Easter Island worried about whether the trees they chopped down for firewood might contribute to a desolate, bleak landscape for their descendants.

But when the river of prices starts to rise and the profits pour in, the familiar competitive reference points with which to judge the value received will have long been submerged or swept away. Jeff's decision to name the company Amazon—the name of the biggest river in the world, which sweeps away everything in its path—now makes more sense to me.

A focus on ensuring an information advantage was not the only lesson that Jeff learned from Dave Shaw. He also took to heart the immense benefits that advanced computer technology could bring to profiting from this data.

In principle, Amazon could have accomplished much of its success using only traditional retail practices behind the scenes—hiring product managers to monitor competitors and set prices, purchasing agents to select and order inventory, and warehouse workers to pick and ship orders. And indeed Amazon has plenty of all of these. But Jeff also invested heavily and early in automated systems to exploit his unique advantages. These aren't the conventional data-processing systems of bricks-and-mortar competitors, which don't have the opportunity to instantly adjust prices to market conditions and individual customer habits. And that's where artificial intelligence, particularly machine learning systems, comes in.

Continuously testing and adjusting prices on an individual basis while responding to competitive threats is mind-bogglingly complex. Whether your goal is to reinforce the perception of low prices or to maximize profits, extraordinary speed and judgment is required, applied thousands of times a second across countless simultaneous transactions. Conducting this massive ballet requires a synthetic intellect. And that's exactly what Amazon has built.

Are customers willing to pay a penny more for tissue after

their home team loses a closely fought football game? Are buyers in the winning city less sensitive about the price of champagne? Are you likely to purchase a spare iPhone charger at full price if you can get it on Tuesday, or are you the sort of person who needs a slight discount to put you over the edge? Do people who stream classic films before noon prefer reading romances to mysteries on their Kindle? And by exactly how much?

These questions may be difficult to answer, but at least you can detect some glimmer of logic behind them. Even to consider asking them requires a level of insight that few professional human marketers possess. A synthetic intellect, on the other hand, suffers from no such constraints. Perhaps customers with hyphenated names are willing to pay more for artificial flowers on weekdays than on weekends, those who live in apartments prefer books with blue covers to books with red ones, or MasterCard holders are less likely to return earphones if purchased along with other items. This is the unfathomable ocean explored by machine learning algorithms. Here's an actual sample complaint on an Amazon discussion board: "I've been following the 42LV5500 [LG forty-two-inch HDTV], the price drops to 927 over night, then around 9am EST, it pops to 967, then around 5pm it drops between $5–$10, then drops again to 927 overnight. I noticed it in the morning, cancelled my order and repurchased at the 927 price. It is infuriating. They have followed this pattern for 3 days straight."[9]

Today Amazon maintains the illusion, if not the reality, of having everyday low prices. In the future, nothing will deter such companies from presenting you, and only you, with precisely the offers and deals that will maximize the company's profits.

Throughout this process, you will remain thoroughly in control. After all, it's a free country—you can decide for yourself, take it or leave it, choose whatever path strikes your fancy. But while you may exercise freedom as an individual, collectively we will not. Synthetic intellects are fully capable of managing the behavior of groups to a fine statistical precision while permitting individuals to roam in whatever direction their predictable little hearts desire.

Amazon, of course, is simply a single example of a phenomenon that is quietly expanding into many aspects of our lives. Synthetic intellects of every variety discreetly bargain with us, take our measure, and note our interests. But there's a fine line between simply bringing relevant opportunities to our attention and incenting us to take actions that benefit others. And the authority to craft these incentives, and thereby manage our collective behavior, is gradually moving from people to machines.

Today, coupons pop up on your smartphone as you drive past the local mall.[10] Soon, you will wake up to text messages that offer a reserved parking spot close to your office if you agree to leave for work fifteen minutes earlier than usual, give you a free movie ticket if you skip watering your lawn, let you upgrade your iPhone a year sooner if you donate a pint of blood to your health maintenance organization before Friday.[11]

Our lives will be filled with individual propositions like these, managed by synthetic intellects whose goals are to optimize traffic, conserve natural resources, and manage health care. But there will be other systems with less lofty goals—to sell out the last doughnut as close as possible to closing time, to rent you a street-view apartment when a river view is also available, to route you through Salt Lake City while reserving the direct flights for higher-paying last-minute travelers.

But the part of these systems visible to you will only be the snowcap on the mount. Behind the scenes, they will also be furiously negotiating and bartering among themselves to accomplish their goals. How did the water department's resource management system get those Fandango movie ticket coupons? By contracting with another system whose goal is to generate revenue for the movie theaters. How did your HMO's blood plasma inventory system arrange for that iPhone upgrade? By bartering with another system charged with extending cell phone contracts.

The problem, as with the automated securities-trading systems competing in the same forums as human traders, is that you will be incessantly horse-trading with systems that have overwhelming advantages over you: speed; access to timely information; knowledge of exactly what the next person is likely to accept; and the ability to predict your own behavior better than you can. You'll be playing against the house in a game where the dealer counts every card and knows exactly how the deck is sorted. You'll be surrounded by Amazons in all aspects of your life, with no humans in sight.

This is a strange frontier, without precedent in the history of humankind. The new regime will creep in silently and unnoticed, as if on cat paws, while you marvel at how the modern world grows ever more convenient, customized to you, and efficient. But behind the scenes, enormous synthetic intellects will be shaving you the thinnest slice of the benefits that you are willing to accept, while reserving the lion's share for ... exactly whom?

# 7. America, Home of the Brave Pharaohs

n his 1926 short story "The Rich Boy," F. Scott Fitzgerald famously wrote, "Let me tell you about the very rich. They are different from you and me." At the time, his world seemed to be fracturing into three classes—those who could buy and do whatever they wanted, those who were constrained to living on the fruits of their own labor, and those who wished they or their children might someday be in one of the other two groups.

In previous ages, the trappings of class tended to be quite visible. The clothes and jewelry you wore, your accent, which railcar you rode in or deck your stateroom was on broadcast to those around you where you fit into a hierarchy of society largely measured by your material wealth.

But in today's world of blue-jeans-wearing CEOs, twenty-something startup billionaires, private aircraft, and carry-on luggage, identifying the most fortunate among us is a more difficult task. For those at the very top, *Forbes* magazine publishes an annual ranking, simultaneously a source of pride and embarrassment for many on the list. But for an astonishing array of extremely wealthy people, keeping their riches out of sight is something of an obsession.

It's one thing to assert your status among your peers, at the Pebble Beach clubhouse or a Four Seasons resort in Hawaii, but standing out at the local movie theater or your kid's soccer league awards ceremony is another story. People don't like it, and they don't like you. So you're careful to fit in. You don't mention the Porsche Speedster your husband gave you for your twentieth anniversary, the vacation home you just bought on a whim in Carmel, or what your personal trainer said when he stopped by that morning for your daily workout. Better to be discreet.

I'm going to be indiscreet, not to show off but to make an important point. Some of the readers of this book will be nodding in agreement—yep, that's the way I live too. A larger group will likely be put off or possibly appalled. Some will simply find what I have to say so outside their own experience they may doubt my veracity. My only request is that you stay tuned for the punch line.

My wife and I live in a nice place. Our home sits on an acre of flat land, graced with majestic oak, redwood, and sycamore trees yet only a short walk from movie theaters, parks, fine restaurants, and just about every imaginable amenity and service. Just before sundown, hundreds of crows often flock to our giant sycamore for a raucous gabfest before turning in for the night, no doubt to discuss their murderous ways. Mated pairs of mourning doves perch stoically on overhead cables to keep tabs on their offspring, occasionally under the watchful eye of a majestic red-tailed California hawk. Bored? You can sit in the graceful Adirondack chairs around the fire pit, play chess on a life-sized outdoor chess board, laze in the gazebo by the pool, take a dip in the hot tub, cook on the outdoor barbeque, relax on the porch swing, play croquet on the front lawn, or stroll through the manicured gardens that brim with multicolored roses for much of the year. Like to listen to music outdoors? There are two separate high-quality sound systems concealed in different areas.

Our house was built in 1904 by a famous architect in the Georgian style. The first floor has ten-foot ceilings in a forty-by-twenty-five-foot living room, a billiard room, a theater room with projection system decorated like a Viennese bordello, a kitchen with four different sitting areas, two refrigerators, two microwaves, two sinks, and three dishwashers, all of which come in handy for parties. But the real jewel is the dining room. It was purchased in Europe by a previous resident, who had it disassembled and reconstructed on site. It sports dark wood paneling, a unique Jacobean floral design on the plaster ceiling, and an original cast-iron fireback dated 1606. Seats up to twenty-four comfortably for dinner. The second floor contains five separate suites, one for each of our four kids and a larger one for us, incorporating a second projection theater system. The third floor has my office, a workout room, and a guest suite with two bedrooms and a bath with an original claw-foot freestanding tub. Almost forgot to mention the wine cellar and elevator.

We can handle about 150 people in the house for a party without breaking a sweat. But for larger groups, we need to use the guesthouse. This two-story structure in the style of a New England farmhouse has two baths, three bedrooms, three refrigerators, two kitchens, and an open downstairs floor plan that can accommodate around 200 guests.

I'm sincerely, truly grateful for my life, and particularly for my wife. I am thankful for my family, my friends, and the freedom to basically do whatever I want with my remaining years, like playing piano and writing this book. Believe me, it hasn't always been like this. I've lived in tenements on the South Side of Chicago, been beaten and robbed at knifepoint, taken the subway home from my warehouse job in Brooklyn to a roach-infested studio rental in sub-freezing temperatures.

You've been very patient, so here's the punch line: according to the latest statistics, based on income, we're not even in the fabled top 1 percent of Americans. That is to say, more than one out of a hundred people earn more each year than we do, and presumably live higher on the proverbial hog.[1]

And I know plenty of people who make us look like paupers. One of our friends owns seven residential properties, including a ranch, houses in Big Sur, Sun Valley, and Puerto Vallarta, and fifty-three acres of prime Pacific oceanfront property a short drive from his main palatial residence in Silicon Valley. Other neighbors have horse stables, jogging trails, and collections of antique cars. There's one house a short distance from us that's over thirty thousand square feet set on six acres, with both indoor and outdoor lap pools and a chapel with a full-sized pipe organ. Paul Simon performed as the entertainment for one friend's private birthday party. Some have not one private jet but two—in case one family member wants to spend the weekend in Aspen while the other prefers Palm Springs. Another bought a ten-story hotel and several surrounding downtown buildings to start his own private school for entrepreneurship, as a hobby. Some host fund-raisers for a parade of supplicating politicians, including sitting and former presidents.

By contrast, I do my own laundry each weekend. My wife does the dishes and takes the kids to and from school every day. I drive a fifteen-year-old car because the damn thing just won't break down. (Don't buy a Lexus—they are too well made and last too long.) My wife doesn't care much for expensive jewelry, so she's happy to wear earrings from Claire's, a store that sells shiny baubles to teenagers.

But even our wealthier friends and neighbors aren't among the richest in the land—most don't come close to qualifying for the Forbes list. That honor is reserved for people with multiple billions of dollars.

Jeff Bezos is on this list, with a personal fortune estimated by

Forbes at $32 billion (as of March 2011). What does that number mean? Let's assume an 11 percent annual return, which is the average return on equities over the past fifty years. That's $3.5 billion a year in appreciation, or $9.6 million per day, including weekends.

By comparison, the average *lifetime* earnings of a U.S. college graduate is $2.3 million, and the average high school graduate earns about $1.3 million.[2] Jeff makes more on a Saturday spent on the golf course than the other college grads in his foursome, taken together, will earn in their entire lifetimes.

Here's a more disturbing comparison. In the depths of the recent recession (2009), the California state budget ran a deficit of $26.3 billion, far less than Jeff Bezos's net worth.[3] Efforts to close this gap in subsequent years included pay cuts and forced furloughs for state workers of three days a month, approximately a 10 percent reduction in K–12 and community college funding, a shortened school year, early prison releases and summary parole, and reductions in the Medi-Cal program. These cuts disproportionately affected the aged, blind, disabled, children, preschool programs, emergency food assistance, pregnant women, and women enrolled in the California Breast and Cervical Cancer Treatment Program (BCCTP), to name a few.[4]

In no way am I suggesting that Jeff didn't earn or does not deserve his wealth. He's certainly not in any way responsible for California's budget challenges and governance failures. On the contrary, in his spare time, he supports a number of projects and programs that serve the public interest. For instance, he gave $15 million for brain research at Princeton University and $20 million to the Hutchinson Cancer Research Center.[5]

But, as with increasing computing power, at some point, quantitative differences become qualitative. Having more than a few tens of millions of dollars under your control today doesn't affect your lifestyle or your ability to help out friends and relatives in a pinch. It gives you power. The power to sway elections, influence politicians and legislation, impact the public agenda—but mostly, the power to divert society's resources toward matters of personal interest to you.

For instance, Jeff Bezos started Blue Origin, a company working to reduce the cost of spaceflight so private individuals (as opposed to governments) can explore the solar system. This is laudable, and it's certainly his right to do it, but might the resources devoted to this high-minded effort be better applied elsewhere, or perhaps be directed by more than a single individual's passions? Steven A. Edwards, a policy analyst at the American Association for the Advancement of Science, remarked, "For better or worse, the practice of science in the 21st century is becoming shaped less by national priorities or by peer-review groups and more by the particular preferences of individuals with huge amounts of money."[6]

Tourists in Seattle in 2000 may have been delighted by a visit to the Experience Music Project Museum, originally inspired by and dedicated to Jimi Hendrix, but they might wonder why the city hosted an $80 million homage to this particular pop artist rather than his equally talented deceased contemporaries like Janis Joplin or Jim Morrison, much less great American composers like Aaron Copland or George Gershwin.[7] Having jammed with Paul Allen, cofounder of Microsoft, on guitar, it's no mystery to me. He loves and emulates Jimi Hendrix's playing style (and I might add is very good at it), which is why he personally financed this particular civic project.

The list of wealthy people who have purchased or supported sports teams, or even whole sports, seems endless. For instance, Oracle's CEO Larry Ellison invested $300 million in the America's Cup yacht race. Thom Weisel, founder of Montgomery Securities, personally organized a bailout of USA Cycling, the governing body for U.S. bicycle racing, in 2000.

There's a widespread belief that for the economy to thrive, we need a robust and healthy middle class. The reasoning is that there needs to be strong demand for consumer goods, and who would buy them if not the middle class? Unfortunately this is completely mistaken.

For much of its existence, ancient Egypt was ruled by a single absolute monarch. The pharaoh, believed to literally be the child of the sun god Ra, personally owned all the resources of the kingdom. A large bureaucracy of administrators and clergy administered the distribution of land and collection of taxes on the pharaoh's behalf. During many critical periods, after meeting the minimum physical needs of the public for food and shelter, much of Egypt's excess wealth went into construction of a single monolithic building—a pyramid to serve as the pharaoh's tomb. These magnificent structures, coated with highly polished white limestone, likely gleamed so brightly in the midday sun that one was forced to avert one's eyes. The size of the workforce required to build one of the larger pyramids is in dispute, but most modern scientific estimates peg it at around twenty-five thousand workers laboring for a sustained period of two or more decades.[8]

You might think that this sort of wasteful endeavor in the service of a single person might cause an empire to collapse under the threat of violent revolution. But ancient Egypt had a relatively stable political and economic system for several thousand years, something that seems almost beyond hope for modern political entities.

A common misconception is that these workers were slaves. On the contrary, there is ample evidence that they were volunteers, or at least citizens fulfilling compulsory public-service requirements. In contrast to much of the population, they mostly dined on meat.

For much of the relevant time frame, the population of ancient Egypt was around 1.5 million. A proportionately comparable workforce in the United States today to the one that built the pyramids would be about 5 million workers. To put this in perspective, the United States has about 1.5 million active-duty military personnel, second only to China. At its peak in 1967, NASA's U.S. space program employed thirty-six thousand people.[9] Walmart is the largest private employer in the United States, with 1.3 million domestic workers.

It's hard to imagine 5 million people working on the pet project of some Internet mogul, particularly because the cost would be in the tens or hundreds of billions of dollars annually. But ten times this number could work for the wealthiest 1 percent of U.S. households on a continuing basis. And increasingly, that's what happening.

The top 1 percent of households cumulatively hold slightly more than one-third of the total wealth in the United States. That pencils out to about $20 trillion. Assuming an annual rate of return of 10 percent, they could afford to spend $2 trillion a year, every year, on whatever they want. At the U.S. worker's median salary of approximately $30,000, this would employ over 60 million people, or 40 percent of the total workforce. At an average salary of $20,000, which is currently earned by nearly 40 percent of the workforce, the wealthiest 1 percent could employ two out of every three workers in the United States.[10] Presumably the rest would be needed to provide the basics for those lucky enough to land a job working for the rich.

What might this look like? As with most such stark pictures, it's not realistic. Two out of three people wouldn't be commuting to private homes to rub the feet of the rich. But the truth isn't as far distant from this scenario as you might hope.

The first reason this isn't happening is that the wealthy aren't spending all they could—not by a long shot. This money is being reinvested and put to other uses, with the returns piling up in personal "rainy day," trust, and retirement funds. This is the proverbial rich getting richer.

The second reason is that you can't see most of the labor devoted to the whims of the rich because it is embodied in goods and services. If my wife purchases a Gucci handbag for $1,000, that money is going in two directions. Gucci shareholders are getting about $300, but the remaining $700 is going mainly to pay people to make it, either directly (that is, as employees of Gucci) or indirectly to their suppliers' employees.[11] Piercing this dance of the corporate veils, the entire labor force making the bag is, for all practical purposes, working for my wife and others like her. What would a similar bag cost if made as cheaply as possible? That's an easy question to answer because a visually indistinguishable knockoff costs around $30 (including profit). Of course, you can get an equally practical handbag for even less at Sears. Therefore, roughly speaking, about $650 of that purchase is going not to the practical utility of being able to carry personal items around but to the maintenance of social status and the personal sense of self-worth generated through the display of gratuitous expenditure.

One way to see how the wealthy are reshaping our economy is to look at sales growth of these so-called luxury items. While the latest economic downturn certainly had an impact, the general consensus among industry analysts is that consumer demand for luxury brands is recession-proof.[12] According to a report from the Carlyle Group, global sales for luxury apparel, accessories, and goods have experienced double-digit annual growth every year since 2009 and are expected to be four times the projected European GDP growth for the next three years. Bain & Company reports that the highest 2013 luxury segment growth was in the Americas, surpassing China, the previous leader.[13]

When the growth rate of luxury goods consistently exceeds the growth rate for all retail sales, it doesn't take long for it to account for a large proportion of total spending. According to Mark Zandi, chief economist of Moody's Analytics, the top 5 percent of income earners account for about one-third of all spending, and the top 20 percent account for close to 60 percent of spending.[14] It's quite plausible that, within the next decade, the wealthiest 5 percent could generate more than half of retail spending in the United States. That would be a thriving economy driven not by the mythical middle class but rather by an ever-concentrating cadre of the elite.

It's uncomfortable to realize that Jeff Bezos alone, with the stroke of a pen, could have wiped out the 2009 California annual deficit and still have had several billion dollars left to enjoy. I can't speak for Jeff, but were I in that position, I would sleep a bit less soundly at night. How many lives could I save? How much suffering could I alleviate? How many dreams fulfill?

The superwealthy carry a burden, wittingly or not, that the rest of us do not. Many come to realize that charitable endeavors are a moral imperative that they cannot or should not ignore, regardless of what they might personally prefer to do with their time and money. Bill Gates is an example that comes to mind. Even I have misgivings when I contribute to my kid's private school capital campaigns instead of a local homeless shelter. We are all faced with choices, and tax deductibility does not indicate righteousness.

Another affliction unique to the rich is the erosion of meaning in their lives. When everything is freely available, nothing has value. When you don't have to strive to acquire something you covet, when you can buy your way out of uncomfortable situations and aren't forced to compromise with others, you lose the psychological boundaries that give shape to your life. One thing I've noticed when my friends "make it" is that their emotional growth tends to cease. Their level of personal maturity is frozen in time like an insect in amber, for all to see. Recognizing this risk, one of my most successful and accomplished friends, a star partner at a top-tier venture capital firm, segregates his day-to-day living expenses from his enormous wealth, which he consciously ignores by leaving its management to others. He prefers to live a relatively modest, though comfortable, lifestyle.[15]

But enough about the rich. Let's look at the other side of this coin—the myriad of talented people who work hard yet struggle all their lives for simple things that the elite take for granted. It's easy to display statistics and charts showing just how difficult life is for the working poor, much less the nonworking poor. But somehow these tools don't capture the real gravity of their circumstances. So instead, I've selected a single individual—typical in many ways—to profile, in the hope that his story will convey these struggles more graphically.

Emmie Nastor is the perfect employee. I know, because I hired him. In 2009, I was running a small Internet game company called Winster.com. When we grew to about ten employees, it was clear we needed a receptionist. The job required good computer and people skills, a pleasing demeanor, and a willingness to do a wide variety of randomly assigned tasks. So I asked my overworked office manager to post a job on Craigslist.

A few days later, I asked her how the search was coming. "Terrible. I've gotten over 250 résumés. Just to read through them is going to take most of the day. And they're still coming in." This was a big surprise because even during the recession, you had to lure software engineers to interviews with promises of hefty salaries and generous stock-option packages. I instructed her to review the first hundred or so, select a dozen to discuss with me, and ignore the rest.

When I reviewed the résumés I was aghast. Most applicants were grossly overqualified for this entry-level job, which offered a starting salary of $29,000 per year. There were MBAs from local universities, homemakers attempting to return to work with years of obsolete experience under their belts, and people with extensive skills in some irrelevant specialty, all plainly desperate for any paid position. Some offered to work for free for a while to demonstrate their abilities; others simply promised that they would stoically accept their reduced circumstances indefinitely if only we would give them a chance.

As sad as this was, I knew that there was no point in hiring someone who would be unhappy with the work and constantly on the prowl for a better opportunity. So I selected two or three candidates with appropriate credentials to bring in for interviews.

It was a tough choice, but Emmie's strong skills with Microsoft Office and his thoughtful and direct responses to my questions won him the job.

What I didn't know at the time was the path he took to arriving on my doorstep. Emmie was born and raised in California, son of a hard-working immigrant couple. His parents emigrated to the United States after his father enlisted in the U.S. Air Force and worked as a mechanic back in the Philippines. Eventually he got a job installing telephone lines in people's homes with a major telecommunications company. Emmie grew up in Daly City, a working-class suburb south of San Francisco, along with an older sister and younger brother. He graduated from Westmoor High in 1994.

His parents were staunch believers in the American dream and felt strongly that a college education was the ticket to a better life. The most practical way for Emmie to achieve this goal was to enroll in a local community college. After four years of attending classes while working part-time jobs, Emmie was able to transfer to San Francisco State University. After another four years, at the ripe old age of twenty-eight, he fulfilled his parents' aspirations for him, earning a college degree. (Unfortunately, his mother never lived to see it. She died of colon cancer in 2007 after a protracted illness.)

Armed with his new degree, he set out to find a full-time job. With his characteristic diligence, he would spend at least eight hours each day scanning the Internet for opportunities, composing cover letters, and sending out résumés—usually twenty to thirty a day. He did this nonstop for three months straight. Five to seven days a week, twenty to thirty résumés a day for three months works out to over eighteen hundred job applications—without so much as a single invitation to interview.

Now, some people might have gotten a tad discouraged and stopped looking for work. But not Emmie. In addition to the usual motivations, what kept him going was his understanding with his childhood sweetheart that they would get married only after he was bringing home a regular paycheck. So failure was not an option.

Then suddenly he got a break. Actually, two breaks at the same time. We called him in to interview for the receptionist job, and Enterprise Rent-a-Car tapped him for a position as a sales management trainee.

As luck would have it, a friend of his who was already working for Enterprise could offer some insight into the position. The title sounded good, but the job required him to put in ten or more hours a day for basically the same salary that Winster was offering for eight. Even worse, he would have no control over his schedule. The company could require him to work any random hours, day or night, seven days a week, entirely at its discretion. He would be eligible for a promotion after he delivered a certain level of sales, but there were no guarantees. So Emmie accepted the offer from Winster.

Emmie never voluntarily missed a day of work. I say this because he would occasionally show up sneezing and coughing, and we would send him home for the sake of everyone else in the office. You could set the office clock by his prompt arrival at 9:00, and if there was anything left to be done at the end of the day he would stay to complete it. No task was beneath him. Cleaning up after weekly company lunches, running to Staples for an odd cable, selecting a get-well card for a sick employee—Emmie was up for it all. I could never persuade him that he didn't need to ask permission to go to lunch.

At one point, I was surprised to learn that his car was in the shop for an indefinite stay. It had blown a timing belt, and he couldn't afford to pay the $500 repair until his paycheck cleared. How did he get to work? Since he was the main breadwinner in the household at that point, his family decided that his younger brother would have to miss school so Emmie could use his car.

In mid-2012, we sold Winster to another game company, and Emmie's position was eliminated (along with mine). So Emmie went back to searching for a job. I wrote him a stellar recommendation, of course, but it turned out not to matter—no one cared to even ask for it. This time, things were a little easier. He spent only two months sending out résumés before he got an expression of interest, from the same telecommunications company his father had worked for, to become a premises installer. This was basically an updated version of the job his father had wiring up people's homes, but this time for cable and Internet in addition to telephone service.

Soon after applying, he learned that there were over a hundred applicants for the same position. To be considered for the job, he first had to pass a two-hour competency test. This covered not the usual high school math or English but rather the applicant's knowledge of wiring standards and installation practices. In other words, you had no hope of landing the position unless you already had the specific skills required or the diligence to learn the subject on your own (the company provided no training materials in advance). Emmie's big advantage was that his father could tutor him on the subject.

But that wasn't the end of the process. Next, fifty or more people were called back for face-to-face interviews. When Emmie's turn came, he was questioned by two different people for about ten minutes each. He must have made the cut, because he was then instructed to report to a medical facility for a physical exam and drug test. The company finally offered him the position at a starting annual salary that was $6,500 more than his Winster salary. He was elated to accept.

The job did not turn out to be what he expected. Working conditions mirrored those of nineteenth-century factory workers;

plainly many of the extensive regulatory reforms and safeguards put in place to protect workers are ineffective. He was sometimes required to work six consecutive days a week, often for twelve or fourteen hours a day. Refusal to work these hours was considered "insubordination," which is legalese for grounds for termination. No one in his work group was permitted to go home if customers were still waiting for their promised installation or repair appointment, no matter how late it was. Occasionally he didn't finish work until close to midnight.

He was rarely home before his wife had gone to bed. With about an hour of free time most days, he got to see his family for more than a few minutes only once a week. His last vacation had been shortly after he started at Winster, when he took time off to get married and honeymoon in Hawaii for a few days. That's five years without a break.

Emmie researched positions within the company that might offer him opportunities to learn or get on some sort of career path. But in a Catch-22, he wasn't allowed to apply for an internal transfer without his supervisor's approval, and not one of them—he had five different supervisors during his eighteen-month tenure—was willing to even give him a chance. He was too valuable where he was.

Ever wonder what happens with those annoying customer-satisfaction surveys you are pestered to fill out? If a customer is unhappy with the service, the installer is called in to the office for a reprimand. Unless there's a reasonable excuse, the employee is commonly disciplined with a suspension without pay.

After a year and a half of back-breaking work, crawling under houses and climbing over roofs, Emmie's back actually broke. It happened early in the workday as he was carrying some heavy equipment into a customer's home. In accordance with what he believed was proper procedure, he called his supervisor. There was no answer, so he left a message. In serious pain, be returned to the dispatch depot—but not before completing the installation, for fear of a reprimand. But he got one anyway—for not making more of an effort to reach a supervisor immediately after an on-the-job injury. He was suspended for three days without pay.

During his rehabilitation for sciatica and lower back pain, the company restricted him to "light duty," basically sitting in the office and calling customers to confirm their appointments for the next day. His employers apparently expected him to hate this and quit, but they don't know Emmie. He soldiered on with his characteristic upbeat demeanor. But the temporary respite gave him time to ponder what his newborn son's life might be like if he grows up in a household where Dad is never around. So he took the opportunity to see what opportunities with saner hours might be available. After once again sending out a blizzard of résumés, he finally got a bite ... from Enterprise Rent-a-Car, before giving up the search in despair.

Despite the appalling working conditions, lack of respect, and dearth of prospects for advancement, Emmie remains grateful for the job and the paycheck. He accepts with equanimity the broken promise that his eight-year slog to get a college degree would offer a path to a life better than his father's.

What happened to his dad? After retiring a few years ago, he decided that he didn't like retirement, so he landed a job with his old employer as a premises installer—at half his previous salary. Even worse, the position was in Sacramento. After suffering through a multihour commute for about a year, he decided to pull up stakes and move, leaving his house in Daly City to Emmie and his siblings.

Emmie is happy for his dad. He also regards himself as lucky to inherit a partial interest in the house his father was able to purchase decades ago with savings accumulated by working at essentially the same job that Emmie has now. Without this, there's no way he could possibly hope to set aside enough for a down payment on a similar property, much less qualify for a mortgage, particularly considering the mountain of student loan debt he'll be paying off for the foreseeable future.

I asked Emmie if he was concerned that my telling his story might affect his employment status. "Not really," he said thoughtfully. "It's very unlikely that anyone I work with would ever read your book."

Like my own story, Emmie's has a punch line. Including his overtime pay and some contributions made by his wife and brother, his household income is well above the national median, $53,046 in 2012. And with his part ownership in the house and some other assets his father is leaving to him, his net worth also far exceeds the median of $77,300 (2010).[16] Which is to say that Emmie and his family are in better financial shape than more than half the households in the United States. Yet he's constantly worried about falling behind. "I can't say that we are better off than others, nor can I say that we are free from having financial issues . . . all that I can say is that we are trying our best to stay afloat in this dog-eat-dog economy. So far, so good."

But the real threat to Emmie's future isn't even on his radar screen yet. It seems obvious that his assignment confirming customer's appointments can be easily automated. But his entire profession is under threat from technical advances in wide-area high-bandwidth wireless communication. These systems use enormous computing power and sophisticated adaptive AI algorithms to continuously adjust radio signals to local conditions at multiple receivers simultaneously, eliminating the need for on-premises wiring entirely.[17]

One such technology is DIDO (distributed input, distributed output), developed by Silicon Valley entrepreneur Steve Perlman, whose previous accomplishments include QuickTime and WebTV. If his approach wins out in the marketplace, he will add handsomely to his already vast fortune, while the 250,000 people currently employed installing and repairing wiring in the United States will be applying for entry-level jobs with Enterprise Rent-a-Car.[18]

# 8. Take This Job and Automate It

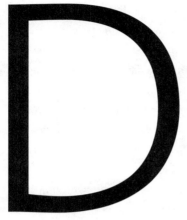espite what you read in the press, global warming isn't all bad, and certainly not for everyone. There will be winners and losers, depending on where you live. In my case, it's a tad too cool around here for my taste, but luckily for me, the average temperature where I live is projected to rise several degrees over the next few decades. Sounds good; hope I live to see it.

Global warming in and of itself isn't a problem. After all, life on earth has survived numerous cycles of cooling and heating. The real problem with global warming is how quickly it happens. If there isn't enough time for living things (including us) to adapt, rapid changes in climate, not to mention more volatile weather patterns, can sow havoc. The consequences of catastrophic climate change can reverberate for centuries as species suffer horrific losses of their habitat, leading to mass extinctions.

The impact of technological change on our labor markets works the same way. As long as change is gradual, the markets can respond. Too fast, and it's chaos. And as with my particular environmental preferences, it creates winners and losers.

The likely accelerating effect of recent advances in artificial intelligence on technological change is going to roil our labor markets in two fundamental ways. The first is the simple truth that most automation replaces workers, so it eliminates jobs. That means fewer places for people to work. This threat is easy to see and measure—employers roll in a robot and walk a worker to the door. But sometimes change is less visible. Each new workstation may eliminate the need for one-fifth of a salesperson, or free Skype calls may allow you to work more productively at home one day a week, deferring the need for that new hire until next quarter.

If this happens slowly, the resulting improvements in productivity and reduced cost eventually create wealth, stimulating job growth that compensates for the losses. The growth may be directly in the newly improved enterprise, as lower prices and better quality increase sales, creating a need to hire more workers. Or it may be in distant parts of the economy where the customers who no longer need to pay as much for some product or service decide to spend the money they saved. If new drilling technologies cause natural gas prices to drop, there's more left over from your paycheck to save for that sailboat you've got your eye on.

But the second threat is much more subtle and difficult to predict. Many technological advances change the rules of the game by permitting businesses to reorganize and reengineer the way they operate. These organizational and process improvements often make obsolete not only jobs but skills. A teller may get laid off when a bank installs ATMs; the improved service creates a need to hire network engineers but not tellers. Even if the bank ultimately expands its total workforce, the tellers remain out of luck. Weavers can eventually learn to operate looms, gardeners to service lawnmowers, and doctors to use computers to select the right antibiotics—once they accept that synthetic intellects are superior to their own professional judgment. But learning the new skills doesn't happen overnight, and sometimes the redundant workers simply aren't capable of adapting—that will have to wait for a new generation of workers.

For an example of labor market transformation that we have weathered successfully, consider agriculture. As recently as the early 1800s, farms employed a remarkable 80 percent of U.S. workers.[1] Consider what this means. Producing food was by far the dominant thing people did for a living, and no doubt this pattern had been typical since the invention of agriculture about five thousand years ago.

But by 1900, that figure had dropped in half, to 40 percent, and today it's only 1.5 percent, including unpaid family and undocumented workers.[2] Basically, we managed to automate nearly everyone out of a job, but instead of causing widespread unemployment, we freed people up for a host of other productive and wealth-producing activities. So over the last two centuries the U.S. economy was able to absorb on average about 1/2 percent loss of agricultural job opportunities each year without any obvious dislocations.

Now imagine that this had happened in two decades instead of two centuries. Your father worked on a farm, and his father before him, as far back as anyone could remember. Then a Henry Ford of farming revolutionized the entire industry in what seemed like a flash. The ground shook with the rumble of shiny new plows, threshers, and harvesters; the air was thick with the smell of diesel. Food prices plummeted, and corporations bought up farmland everywhere with the backing of deep-pocketed Wall Street financiers. Within a few years, your family's farm was lost to foreclosure, along with every possession except the family Bible.

You and your five brothers and sisters, with an average third-grade education, found your skills of shoeing horses, plowing straight furrows, and baling hay utterly useless, as did all of your neighbors. But you still had to eat. You knew someone who knew someone who operated one of the new machines twelve hours a day in return for three squares, who supposedly got the job in Topeka, so you moved to one of the vast tent cities ringing the major Midwestern cities in the hope of finding work—any kind of work. Before long, you got word that your parents sold the Bible to buy medicine for your youngest sister, but she died of dysentery anyway. Eventually you lost track of the rest of your other siblings.

The 1 percent who still had jobs lived in tiny tract houses and barely got by, but they were nonetheless the envy of the rest—at least they had a solid roof over their heads. Each day, you waited in line outside their gated communities hoping for a chance to wash their clothes or deliver their bag lunches. Rumors spread that the daughters of the storied entrepreneur who changed the world had used his vast fortune to build a fabulous art museum made of crystal in a small town in Arkansas. But all this was before the revolution. After that, things got really bad.

I'm going to argue that a similarly tectonic shift looms ahead, though doubtlessly less dramatic and more humane. Forged laborers will displace the need for most skilled labor; synthetic intellects will largely supplant the skilled trades of the educated. When initially deployed, many new technologies will substitute directly for workers, getting the job done pretty much the same way. But other innovations will not only idle the workers; they will eliminate the types of jobs that they perform.

For example, consider the way Amazon constantly adapts the stock patterns in its warehouses. If a person were to do the warehouse planning (as in many more traditional companies), products might be organized in a logical and comprehensible way—identical items would be stored next to each other, for example, so when you needed to pick one, you knew where it was. But a synthetic intellect of the sort Amazon has built isn't subject to this constraint. Like items can be located next to others that are frequently shipped with them, or on any shelf where they fit more compactly. To the human eye, it looks like chaos—products of different sizes and shapes are stacked randomly everywhere—which is why this type of warehouse organization is known as chaotic storage.[3] But a synthetic intellect can keep track of everything and direct a worker to exactly the right place to fulfill an order far more efficiently than a human organizer could.

A side effect of introducing this innovation is that it reduces the training and knowledge required of warehouse workers, making them more susceptible to replacement by forged laborers. These employees no longer have to be familiar with the location of products on the shelves; indeed, it would be near impossible to do so in such a haphazard and evolving environment. Having first simplified the skills required to get the job done, Amazon can now replace the workers that roam the warehouse floor picking those orders. This is likely why the company bought the robotics company Kiva Systems, reportedly for $775 million, in 2012.[4]

This is a single example of a profound shift that synthetic intellects will cause in our world. The need to impose order—not only for warehouses but for just about everything—is driven by the limitations of the human mind. Synthetic intellects suffer no such constraint, and their impact will turn tidiness to turmoil in many aspects of our lives. Our efforts to tame our intellectual and physical domains into manicured gardens will give way to tangled thickets, impenetrable by us.

When most people think about automation, they usually have

in mind only the simple replacement of labor or improving workers' speed or productivity, not the more extensive disruption caused by process reengineering. That's why some jobs that you might least expect to succumb to automation may nonetheless disappear.

For instance, studies often cite jobs that require good people skills or powers of persuasion as examples of ones unlikely to be automated in the foreseeable future. But this isn't necessarily the case. (As I noted in chapter 4, the CEO of Rocket Fuel observed that persuasion was a skill that his company's ad placement service largely replaces.)

The ability to convince you that you look terrific in a particular outfit is certainly the hallmark of a successful salesperson. But why do you need that person when you can ask hundreds of real people? Imagine a clothing store where you are photographed in several different outfits, and the images are immediately (and anonymously, by obscuring your face) posted to a special website where visitors can offer their opinion as to which one makes you look slimmer. Within seconds, you get objective, statistically reliable feedback from impartial strangers, who earn points if you complete a purchase. (This concept is called "crowdsourcing.") Why put your faith in a salesperson motivated by commission when you can find out for sure?

Reflecting these two different effects of automation on labor (replacing workers and rendering skills obsolete), economists have two different names for the resulting unemployment. The first is "cyclical," meaning that people are cycling in and out of jobs.[5] In bad times, the pool of people who are between jobs may grow, leading to higher unemployment. But historically, as soon as the economy picks up, the idled workers find new jobs. Fewer people are unemployed and for shorter periods of time. This works just like the housing market: in a slow market, there are more houses available and the ones that are take longer to sell. But when the market turns around this excess inventory is quickly absorbed.

I was surprised to learn just how much turnover there is in the U.S. labor market. In 2013, a fairly typical year, 40 percent of workers changed jobs.[6] That's a very fluid market. By contrast, less than 4 percent of homes are sold each year.[7] So when we talk about 8 percent unemployment, it doesn't take long for small changes in the rates of job creation and destruction to soak that up, or conversely to spill more people out of work.

The other type of unemployment is called "structural," which means that some group of unemployed simply can't find suitable employment at all. They can send out résumés all day long, but no one wants to hire them, because their skills are a poor match for the available jobs.[8] The equivalent in the housing market would be if the types of houses available weren't suitable for the available buyers. Suddenly couples start having triplets instead of single kids and so need more bedrooms, or people start commuting to work in flying cars that can take off only from flat rooftops, while most houses have pitched roofs.

As you can see from my fanciful examples, the factors that change the desirability of housing don't usually change very fast, so builders and remodelers have plenty of time to adapt. But this isn't true for automation because the pace of invention and the rate of adoption can change quickly and unpredictably, shifting the character of whole labor market segments far more rapidly than people can learn new skills—if they can be retrained at all. We're buffeted about by these fickle winds precisely because they are hard to anticipate and virtually impossible to measure.

Economists and academics who study labor markets have a natural bias toward the quantifiable. This is understandable, because to credibly sound the alarm, they must have the hard data to back it up. Their work must stand up to objective, independent peer review, which basically means it must be reduced to numbers. But as I learned in business, spreadsheets and financial statements can capture only certain things, while trends that resist reduction to measurement often dominate the outcome. (Indeed, there's an argument to be made that the troublesome and unpredictable business cycles plaguing our economy are largely driven by the fact that returns are easily quantified, but risks are not.) I can't count the number of meticulously detailed yet bogus sales projections I've seen bamboozle management teams. At work I sometimes felt my most important contribution as a manager was anticipating that which had yet to manifest itself in quantifiable form.

But talking about the overall labor market, unemployment statistics, or the aggregate rate of change obscures the reality of the situation because the landscape of useful skills shifts erratically. The complexity of this web of disappearing labor habitats and evolving job ecosystems resists analysis by traditional mathematical tools, which is why attempts to quantify this whole process tend to bog down in reams of charts and tables or devolve into hand-waving.

Luckily I'm not bound by these same professional constraints, so fasten your seat belt for a quick tour of the future. My approach will be to look at some specific examples, then attempt to reason by analogy to get a broader picture. Let's start with retail—the largest commercial job market, as determined by the U.S. Bureau of Labor Statistics (BLS).[9]

The BLS reports that about 10 percent of all U.S. workers are employed in retailing, or approximately 14.5 million people.[10] To analyze trends, let's use salespersons as a proxy for the whole group. The BLS projects that this labor force, which stood at 4.4 million in 2012, will grow by 10 percent to 4.9 million over the next ten years. But this is based on current demographic trends, not a qualitative analysis of what's actually going on in the industry.

To get a sense of what's really going to happen, consider the effect on employment of the transition from bricks-and-mortar stores to online retailers. A useful way to analyze this is to use a statistic called revenue per employee. You take the total annual revenue of a company and divide it by the number of employees. It's a standard measure of how efficient a company is, or at least how labor-efficient.

Average revenue per employee for Amazon (the largest online retailer) over the past five years is around $855,000.[11] Compare that to Walmart (the largest bricks-and-mortar retailer), whose revenue per employee is around $213,000—one of the highest of any retailer. This means that for each $1 million in sales, Walmart employs about five people. But for the same amount of sales, Amazon employs slightly more than one person. So for every $1 million in sales that shift from Walmart to Amazon, four jobs are potentially lost.

Now, both companies sell pretty much the same stuff. And Walmart does a good portion of its sales online as well, so the job loss implied by the shift to online sales is understated. And neither company is standing still; both are likely to grow more efficient in the future.

To establish an upper bound on job losses, imagine that magically all retail sales were to suddenly shift from Walmart-like stores to Amazon-like websites. The 10 percent of the labor force (mostly) working in stores would be replaced by 2 percent of the labor force working for online retailers. That's 8 percent fewer jobs available in the United States, more than the entire 2014 unemployment rate. So are we in big trouble here? Not really. Of course, all sales aren't going to shift online—your favorite mall isn't going to close down—and certainly the shift is going to take some time. But how long?

Despite all the hoopla, only 6 percent of U.S. retail sales are currently online. These have been growing consistently at a rate of about 15 percent annually for the past four years.[12] If online sales were to continue to grow at that pace for the next twenty years (unlikely), and if all growth in retail sales went to the online segment (also unlikely), they would then account for at most half of all retail sales. That means that retail sales would have roughly doubled over that period, which is pretty much what they did over the previous two decades, but only 10 percent more people would be required to support these sales.[13] And that assumes that bricks-and-mortar stores don't grow at all, which is not plausible.

Meanwhile, what's going to happen to the labor force? Based on careful demographic projections, the BLS estimates that the labor force will grow only about 12 percent over the next twenty years.[14] In other words, a tremendous shift from bricks-and-mortar stores to far more labor-efficient online retailers will likely result in only a 2 percent negative impact on employment over that period. (That is, the 12 percent labor market growth only slightly exceeds the 10 percent more retail workers required.) That's only .1 percent per year for the economy to absorb, compared to the .5 percent average annual loss of agricultural jobs over the last two centuries. But the story gets better. Surely with a doubling of retail sales, new jobs in all sorts of industries that design, manufacture, and ship these products will more than take up that slack.

Oops, did I include shipping on that list? My mistake. Shipping is a completely different story. In 2012, there were 1.7 million long-haul truck drivers in the United States. These are the people who operate the tractor-trailers and other large cargo-carrying vehicles that frequent the interstate highway system. The BLS projects that the demand for these drivers will grow 11 percent over the next ten years. No way.

While you may regard highway driving as requiring greater skill and more experience than navigating local streets, exactly the opposite is true when it comes to autonomous driving technology, a wonderful hybrid of synthetic intellects and forged laborers. Highways are well maintained, contain fewer random moving obstructions (such as pedestrians and bicycles), and are far more predictable than your local neighborhood streets. The technology to operate self-driving trucks is available today and can be retrofitted to existing fleets at very reasonable costs. Trucks outfitted with such technology can "see" in all directions instead of mostly just straight ahead, drive in complete darkness or blackout conditions, and instantly share information about road conditions, nearby risks, and their own intentions. (Basically, they can rely on detailed 3D radar, called Lidar, in conjunction with detailed maps and GPS, and so have no need for headlights.)

What's more, their reaction time is close to zero. As a result, self-driving trucks can safely caravan with only inches of space between them (called "platooning" in the literature), reducing road congestion and resulting in 15 percent or more fuel savings.[15] Delivery is quicker because they can operate around the clock without rest stops. They don't get tired, drunk, sick, distracted, or bored; they don't doze off, talk on the phone, or go on strike for better wages and working conditions. And how many of the 273,000 large-truck accidents taking 3,800 lives and costing over $4.4 billion (in 2011 alone) could be avoided in the future?[16] May I point out that this single innovation could save more lives annually than were lost in the September 11th World Trade Center disaster?

Such systems aren't futuristic pipe dreams; they are already being tested on real highways and other venues. To quote from a recent press release: "Rio Tinto is rolling out a fleet of 150 automated trucks at our Pilbara iron ore operations, the world's first major deployment of an autonomous truck fleet. Since the two-year trial began, the autonomous trucks have operated every day, 24 hours a day, and have moved more than 42 million tonnes of material in approximately 145,000 cycles. They have travelled more than 450,000 kilometres. We control the trucks from our Operations Centre in Perth, 1,500 kilometres away. The trucks follow pre-defined courses, and GPS systems navigate autonomously from loading units to dump locations."[17]

You don't have to be much of a futurist to see what's coming. Nearly 2 million long-haul truck drivers in ten years? I suspect that the BLS is way off base on this one—more likely closer to zero. But that's only one of the applications for autonomous driving. How many of the more than 5.7 million licensed U.S. commercial drivers (2012) will lose their jobs as a result of variations of this technology?[18] I wouldn't recommend this career option to my kids.

So just based on the aggregate numbers, drivers are probably going to be losing their jobs in droves, but not retail employees. However, there's a twist—the raw numbers obscure a deeper truth. The real issue is not just the overall number of jobs available but the skills required to perform them.

Here's where things get qualitative, so permit me to paint some pictures. There's a big difference between the skills required to sell people things in stores and (for example) those required to maintain an online retailing website. It's not that easy for some kindly grandmother to go from pointing out the location of the shoe department at Walmart to monitoring product reviews at Amazon. A truck driver who may or may not have completed high school and whose main familiarity with computers is watching Netflix may not be well suited for many other jobs, particularly since a wide array of other blue-collar professions are likely to be succumbing to automation as well. Robotic devices that can see and operate in natural environments are about to decimate all sorts of labor markets. Forged laborers, in short, are approaching from all directions. I'll describe a few here.

*Agricultural workers.* Projects are under way that threaten the livelihoods of the remaining 2 to 3 million U.S. farmworkers.[19] In 2010 the European Union started funding the Clever Robots for Crops program (cleverly abbreviated as CROPS). As the project leader explains, "An agricultural robot must be equipped with intelligence so as to be able to robustly operate in the unstructured, dynamic and hostile agricultural environment."[20]

Agrobot, a Spanish company opening an office in Oxnard, California, makes a commercial robot that harvests strawberries.[21] It identifies only the fruit ripe enough for picking. The good news is they're hiring, but only if you've got an engineering degree. I doubt that's much comfort to Elvia Lopez, a kindly thirty-one-year-old Mexican immigrant who picks strawberries in Santa Maria, California (who was profiled in the *Los Angeles Times*).[22] Agrobot isn't alone in tackling this opportunity. A Japanese competitor claims that its technology can reduce strawberry picking time by 40 percent.[23]

Blue River Technologies, a Silicon Valley venture-funded startup headed by a Stanford graduate, is developing robots that can weed. To quote from their marketing materials: "We are creating systems that can distinguish crops from weeds in order to kill the weeds without harming the crops or the environment. Our systems use cameras, computer vision, and machine learning algorithms."[24]

Note that the coming army of mechanical farmworkers doesn't have to be faster than the workers they replace because, like autonomous vehicles, they can work in the dark and so aren't limited to operating in daylight.

*Warehouse workers.* Beyond the picking and packing of orders, as I've described above, there's the loading and unloading of packages. This is done by human workers now because it takes human judgment to decide how to grasp and stack randomly shaped boxes in delivery vehicles and shipping containers. But another Silicon Valley startup, Industrial Perception, Inc., is changing all that. Its robots can peer into a truck, select an item, then pick it up. As it quipped on its website (before the site went dark after the company was acquired by Google in 2013), Industrial Perception is "providing robots with the skills they'll need to succeed in the economy of tomorrow."[25]

*Sex workers.* You'd think prostitution might be a job requiring a human touch. It may be illegal in most of the United States, but sex toys aren't. And they are about to take an entirely new form. Companies like New Jersey–based TrueCompanion are developing full-sized interactive sex dolls in both female and male versions (named Roxxxy and Rocky).[26] As the company founder, Douglas Hines, who previously worked in AI at Bell Labs, said in an interview in 2010, "Artificial intelligence is the underpinning of the whole project." According to the company, "Roxxxy can carry on a discussion and expresses her love to you. She can talk, listen, and feel your touch."[27]

Other projects cooking in AI labs around the world are almost too numerous to mention. They are aimed at tasks like folding laundry, rinsing dishes, then loading them in a dishwasher, bagging groceries, and fetching coffee (one robot even navigates the elevators).[28]

My examples so far may seem to offer some comfort to readers employed in more cerebral endeavors, but this relief would be misplaced. The coming wave of synthetic intellects is going to devastate many of their professions just as surely as forged laborers are going to replace manual laborers. Automation is blind to the color of your collar.

Let's start with the practice of law. The American Bar Association estimates that there were 1.2 million licensed attorneys in the United States in 2010, roughly three-quarters of them in private practice.[29]

There's been much hand-wringing over the challenging economics of getting a professional law degree. It used to be that getting into law school was a great accomplishment, not to mention a ticket on the partner track to the good life. But no more. Applications have been falling year after year as a more practical generation is waking up to economic reality. The Law School Admissions Council reports that applications in 2014 were down nearly 30 percent over just the previous two years, returning to levels last seen in 1977.[30] New graduates can be saddled with debt of more than $150,000, while the average graduate's starting salary in 2011 was only $60,000, down nearly 17 percent from just two years earlier.[31] But they were the lucky ones. In 2009, an astounding 35 percent of newly minted law school graduates failed to find work that required them to pass the bar exam.[32]

There are, of course, many factors affecting job opportunities for attorneys, but automation is certainly among them. And the problems are just getting started. To date, the use of computers in the legal profession has been largely focused on the storage and management of legal documents. This reduces billable hours because you don't have to start from scratch when drafting contracts and briefs. But a new crop of legal-tech entrepreneurs is working to greatly reduce or eliminate the need for lawyers for the most common transactions. In specialty after specialty, innovators are finding that most productive work is sufficiently rote to permit delegation to synthetic intellects. Common commercial contracts, from leases to loans to licenses to incorporation papers to purchase agreements, are well structured enough to allow a first draft, if not a final one, to be written by a computer program.

Consider the legal-tech startup FairDocument.[33] By focusing on estate planning, a well-defined and fairly routine area of law, the company is able to "interview" clients on its website and prepare initial draft documents. Potential clients answer some initial questions, then attorneys bid to get their business. Most of the time, if the case is relatively straightforward, attorneys opt for the standard recommended bid of $995 for an estate plan prepared through Fair-Document, for a service that might otherwise typically cost $3,500 to $5,000.

You might think this simply reduces the lawyer's pay, but attorneys still come out ahead because of what happens next. Instead of conducting the usual phone or in-person interview to educate the new client and collect the needed information, then spending several hours drafting documents, the attorneys let FairDocument walk the client through a lengthy, structured online consultation, explaining the required concepts and collecting the client's particulars. The software then delivers an initial draft to the lawyer, calling out areas that are likely to require his or her additional judgment or attention. Jason Brewster, the company's CEO, estimates that FairDocument reduces the time required to complete a straightforward estate plan from several hours to as little as fifteen to thirty minutes, not to mention that his company is doing the prospecting for new clients and delivering them to the attorneys.

A more sophisticated example of synthetic intellects encroaching on legal expertise is the startup Judicata.[34] The company uses machine learning and natural language processing techniques to convert ordinary text—such as legal principles or specific cases— into structured information that can be used for finding relevant case law. For instance, it could find all cases in which a male Hispanic gay employee successfully sued for wrongful termination by reading the actual text of court decisions, saving countless hours in a law library or using a more traditional electronic search tool.

Other startups are tackling the time-consuming process of early case assessment, discovery processing, document review, document production, and internal investigations.[35] Some do actual legal research and provide advice on case strategy, answering questions like, "How often has a judge ruled in favor of defendants on motions to transfer or motions for summary judgment?" and "What mistakes have tripped up others around similar IP [intellectual property]?"[36]

Some firms are even considering moving the machines from the back room to the nameplate. Consider the cleverly named law firm of Robot, Robot, and Hwang. Yes it's a joke, but the firm is real.

The junior partner, Tim Hwang, has an undergraduate degree from Harvard and a J.D. (law degree) from the University of California at Berkeley. To quote from its website, the firm "attempts to marshal a universe of thinking from the world of technology, startup, and computational science to bear on the often staid and conservative world of legal practice."[37]

Despite efforts by the legal profession to protect its members' livelihoods, an increasing number of startups are bypassing restraints on how and by whom law can be practiced by offering what amounts to automated legal advice presented in different forms over the Internet. For instance, they may employ a small staff of attorneys to "review" documents for correctness before they are released to a client. But most of these startups offer a different format, whereby individual practitioners can be introduced to clients, establish a working (and billing) relationship, then perform their duties with extensive automated support provided by the company.

By offering attorneys the option to work at home, thus avoiding the expense of an office, and by reducing costs through the substitution of sophisticated computer systems for skilled paralegals, these virtual law offices provide an attractive option for practitioners seeking more independence and control over their work. Needless to say, this is an excellent opportunity for graduates who are unable to land an entry-level position at a traditional firm, but it's also attractive to experienced partners who are tired of office politics or of handing over a large proportion of their billings to their firms. These trends are driving down the cost of high-quality legal assistance while improving access for millions of potential clients.

Law schools aren't standing still, though. For instance, a recent course, Legal Informatics, at Stanford University is cotaught by law school and computer science department faculties. The course description says, in part, "What role will lawyers play when customized advice is dispensed over the Internet as easily as cappuccino from a vending machine? Register for a preview of what your job will be like in five years."

If it's less attractive to become a lawyer, how about a doctor? The days of the "country doc" are long gone, but information technology is also transforming the character of medical practitioners in surprising ways.

The main shift is a growing recognition that the medical arts are not arts at all but a science that is better driven by statistics and data than intuition and judgment. In bygone eras, it was at least plausible that someone could absorb a reasonable proportion of the world's medical knowledge and apply it to cases as they are presented. But over the past half century or so, as it became clear that the avalanche of research, clinical trials, and increased understanding of how our bodies (and minds) work was beyond the comprehension of a single individual, the field fractured into a myriad of specialties and practices. Today, your "primary care physician" is more of a travel agent to the land of specialists than a caregiver, except for the simplest of ailments.

But the hidden costs of this divide-and-conquer approach to medical care are about to become painstakingly clear. Coordinating the activities of multiple practitioners into a coherent plan of action is becoming increasingly difficult, for two reasons. First, no one has the complete picture, and, even if they do, they often lack the detailed knowledge required to formulate the best plan of action. Second, specialists tend to treat the specific conditions or body parts that they are trained for, with inadequate regard for the side effects or interactions with other treatments the patient may be receiving. For me, the practice of medicine today conjures the image of a Hieronymus Bosch painting, with tiny, pitchfork-wielding devils inflicting their own unique forms of pain.

As a patient, you would ideally prefer to be treated by a super-doc who is expert in all the specialties and is up to date on all of the latest medical information and best practices. But of course no such human exists.

Enter IBM's Watson program. Fresh off its *Jeopardy!* victory over champions Brad Rutter and Ken Jennings, Watson was immediately redeployed to tackle this new challenge. In 2011, IBM and WellPoint, the nation's largest healthcare benefits manager, entered into a collaboration to apply Watson technology to help improve patient care. The announcement says, "Watson can sift through an equivalent of about one million books or roughly 200 million pages of data, and analyze this information and provide precise responses in less than three seconds. Using this extraordinary capability WellPoint is expected to enable Watson to allow physicians to easily coordinate medical data programmed into Watson with specified patient factors, to help identify the most likely diagnosis and treatment options in complex cases. Watson is expected to serve as a powerful tool in the physician's decision making process."[38] As with its original foray into AI fifty years ago, IBM is still cautious not to ruffle the feathers of the people whose rice bowls they are breaking, but one person's decision process support tool is another's ticket to the unemployment line.

No one likes the idea that his or her field is simply too big and fast moving to master. And doctors in particular aren't likely to graciously concede control of their patients' treatment to synthetic intellects. But eventually, when outcomes demonstrate that this is the better option, patients will demand to see the attentive robot, not the overworked doctor, for a fraction of the fee, just as many people would now rather have an ATM than a human teller count out their cash.

Doctors and lawyers are not the only professionals with much to worry about—there are plenty of others. For instance, today's highly trained commercial pilots should rarely fly planes, particularly if they have the best interests of their passengers in mind. Pilot error is by far the leading cause of fatal crashes, hovering around 50 percent for the past fifty years despite dramatic improvements in air safety.[39] By comparison, mechanical failures are blamed in only 20 percent of events. Planes' autopilots are now so sophisticated that pilots are *required* to use them in certain conditions rather than flying the planes themselves.[40] You may feel some comfort knowing that a trained pilot is standing by in the cockpit in case of a problem, but not if he's feeling blue and decides to crash the plane, as has happened in at least three documented commercial flight accidents in the last twenty-five years that killed everyone on board.[41]

It should be obvious that technologies are capable of replacing teachers and professors in a wide variety of settings. The current buzzword for this is the *flipped classroom*—students watch lectures and learn the material online at home, then do their homework at school with the help of teachers and teaching assistants. Teachers may no longer need to prepare or deliver lectures, reducing them to what could be called "learning coaches." The diminished skill set required is sure to transform the profession and create yet more challenges for our already beleaguered teachers.

But these are anecdotal examples. Just how many professions

will be newly subject to automation in the next decade or so? It's a tough question to answer, but a group of researchers at Oxford University has bravely taken a quantitative approach, matching near-term technologies to job skills required for 702 occupations detailed by the BLS. The researchers' remarkably detailed and insightful analysis reports that 47 percent of total U.S. employment is at high risk of significant automation across a wide variety of blue-collar and white-collar professions. They specifically call out "advances in the fields of ML [machine learning], including Data Mining, Machine Vision, Computational Statistics and other sub-fields of Artificial Intelligence, as well as MR [mobile robotics]" as key drivers of these trends.[42] So an incredible half the workforce, give or take, is in danger of replacement by a machine in the near future.

What's to be done with all these surplus workers with obsolete skills? We need to teach old dogs new tricks—but not just any tricks, tricks that employers will pay them to perform. And the only people who know for sure what tricks these are, are the employers themselves.

With respect to professional training, we are making two mistakes. The first is relying mainly on traditional schools to decide what they should teach students. Our accredited educational institutions are not known for their responsiveness to economic trends, and since the administrators developing the curricula are not customarily out in the field keeping up to date on what novel skills will be most valuable in the economy, they couldn't do it if they wanted to. It's a mystery to me why my kids had to learn penmanship, calculus, and French in high school rather than more practical skills like typing, statistical estimation, and Chinese. (Reading and writing make sense, though.)

Of course, not all educational decisions should be driven by employment prospects. Learning and training are not the same thing. There's plenty of value in raising well-rounded, historically aware, articulate, thoughtful citizens. But beyond a core of basics—which in my opinion doesn't extend to memorizing rows of the periodic table or performing partial differentials—the subject matter should be aimed at equipping students with useful and marketable skills. We should focus on vocational training, not vacational training.

The second mistake is the tacit assumption that first you go to school, and when you are done, you go get a job. This made sense when jobs and skills changed on a generational timescale, but it does not in today's fast-moving labor markets. These two phases of life need to be strongly interleaved, or at least the opportunity for new skill acquisition must be explicit and omnipresent.

The path to addressing both of these issues is through enlightened economic policy. The obvious question regarding the retraining of workers with obsolete skills is who's going to pay. The equally obvious answer is the ones who stand to benefit the most: the workers themselves. But how can down-on-their-luck unemployed workers find and pay for training that matches their abilities and is of real value to employers?

Just as we have special types of loans that are intended to encourage and support homeownership, we need to develop a system of vocational training loans that bear a similar relationship to the targeted asset—in this case, employment rather than houses. When you get a mortgage, the government or the bank that originates it doesn't pay off the loan—you do. If a problem arises, such as your house burns down or you simply can't make the payments, you can walk away and lose only your down payment, because most mortgages are "'nonrecourse" loans, meaning that the only security provided to the lender in the event of default is the property itself. Now, abandoning a house because you can't (or won't) make the monthly payments is certainly painful. You, in addition to the lender, have every incentive to be sure you are a solid credit risk. Both parties also have an incentive to ensure that the property is worth the price being paid (or worth, at least, enough to cover the loan with some margin of safety). This is why lenders require an appraisal supporting the current market value of the house before funding a mortgage.

And similar principles can apply to a vocational training loan. For simplicity, let's call this a job mortgage. Here's at least one way this might work, though there are many variations that could be equally or more effective. To get a job mortgage, you have to se-cure the sponsorship of a potential employer—perhaps the one you are already working for—just as you apply for a mortgage on a par-ticular property. But in this case, the employer isn't promising to hire you, and you aren't promising to take that particular job, though there's a reasonable expectation that if all goes well this is likely to happen. In effect, you are applying for a *future* job, and the employer is issuing a good-faith letter of intent that it has (or will have) a real need to hire someone like you for the position within some reason-able time period.

Because the employer, who is presumably having trouble find-ing workers with appropriate skills, can issue only as many of these sponsorships as it has jobs available, there is a natural limit on the number of people who are able to secure job mortgages. Employers who fulfill their promises can get a tax break (say, relief on payroll taxes for the position for the first six months), which incents them to participate in the program. On the flip side, penalties can be assessed on employers who issue these letters of intent willy-nilly and don't ultimately follow through, within some statistical bounds. A simple way to accomplish this is to require employers to post a modest "bond," which is released only when the position is filled. Employers would also be required to certify that a particular course of training—possibly even one that they themselves provide—will target the needed skills.

Enrollments at the training institutions will be naturally sized to the available pool of jobs in the market, because they are largely reliant on these loans to fund their programs. They are also incented to stay keenly focused on the relevant skills; otherwise the employer(s) will not approve the training as satisfactory for their needs. As a consequence, there is no need for formal government accreditation of these programs—the system is, in effect, self-regulating.

For the potential employee, the key is that the loan is paid back only out of earned income—it is secured by future paychecks. Payments would be limited to some percentage of earnings, say 25 percent of net pay, in a similar spirit to the way mortgage lenders enforce a payment-to-income ratio for their loans. And there needs to be certain built-in relief in case of problems. For example, monthly payments are capped or deferred if the net take-home pay falls below 150 percent of the poverty level established by the government. Because the loan is paid solely from earned income, payments are effectively suspended (though interest may accrue) if the worker is unemployed for any reason, and the loan is automatically reamortized.

What if the training isn't successful, the job isn't available (and no other suitable employment is available either), or the trainee simply decides not to work? As in the case of a home mortgage, the trainee is still responsible for repaying a portion of the loan, say, 20 percent (a typical down payment on a house), regardless of earned income, after a grace period to account for unemployment. That's the way mortgage risk is managed today, and it works just fine.

There are many details that need to be fleshed out, but the basic idea is to create a new type of financial instrument—the job mortgage—through regulations and policies to substitute for or supplement the largely broken current system of student loans, which in many cases saddles innocent victims with debts they can ill afford for inadequate training at for-profit colleges created for the primary purpose of collecting government loan money, with little accountability for the results. Most existing efforts to address this problem have focused on cajoling colleges to do a better job through ratings and other inducements, though recently the government has taken a stronger stand on abusive practices by for-profit institutions, requiring certain graduation rates and employment prospects.[43] But by creating the proper economic incentives for employers, lenders, and trainers through appropriate public policies, we can render the process of skill acquisition and retraining both practical and humane, not to mention much more effective than it is today.

The concept of a job mortgage is a modernized free-market version of the historical apprenticeship or internship model. The main advantage is that it partially decouples the training from the specific employer or position, to great advantage for both the employer and the worker. Instead of the implicit indentured servitude of low-paid trainee positions, which effectively forces companies to operate their own mini-education business and workers to remain at unwanted or inappropriate jobs, people can apply their newly acquired skills where they are most highly valued while employers can draw from an expanded pool of highly skilled workers. This is nothing more than the lubricating role that money is supposed to play in the economy. It's a mystery to me why we seem to treat occupational skills differently than other assets, like some sort of medieval barter system, at great cost to society. If major-league sports figures can securitize their future earnings, why can't the average person do the same?[44]

My specific concept of a job mortgage might be new, but the basic approach certainly isn't. Milton Friedman, leader of the Chicago school of economics, wrote an essay entitled "The Role of Government in Education" in 1955, in which he draws a distinction between "general education for citizenship" and "vocational or professional education." He recommends that the latter should be subject to analysis as an investment, similar to physical assets, and that government policies be put in place to facilitate investment (as opposed to subsidies) in such training. As he put it, "The individual would agree in return to pay to the government in each future year x percent of his earnings in excess of y dollars for each $1,000 that he gets in this way.... An alternative, and a highly desirable one if it is feasible, is to stimulate private arrangements directed toward the same end."[45]

And indeed, today there are some tentative private-sector steps in that direction.[46] For example, Chicago-based Education Equity, Inc., is making income-linked loans to students entering certain approved programs, albeit on a small scale so far.[47]

With this perspective, let's return briefly to the challenges my former employee Emmie Nastor has encountered. In my view, he was utterly failed by our educational system. His B.S. in business administration would seem to be of little practical value, at least in terms of providing the skills that employers in the local job market are actually prepared to pay for. Reportedly, less than half of San Francisco State University's students graduate within six years, and less than half of those secure full-time employment within six months of graduating.[48] (I can find no official statistics on this subject published by the school.) Nonetheless, the university has little incentive other than goodwill to monitor this, much less fix it, as long as students are willing to attend and pay (or take out loans to pay). If to fill its classrooms the university had to meet the collective expectations of local employers, who have every motivation and desire to see the school turn out qualified candidates, it stands to reason that the system would quickly come into equilibrium.

Global warming is a bear, but we aren't bears. Most animals don't have the native intelligence to think their way out of habitat changes, but we do. The accelerating evolution of our labor ecosystem, propelled by continual technological advances, compels us to take a fresh look at the way we prepare our young and even ourselves for productive and fruitful lives.

Excess workers and obsolete skills are a by-product of accelerating economic progress just as surely as greenhouse gases are, and the potential damage to our global labor ecosystem deserves a level of attention comparable to that of climate change. The engines of prosperity, fueled by innovation, are beautiful things to behold—unless you happen to be standing by the tailpipe. Recycling our natural resourcefulness along with our natural resources will surely convey benefits for all.

# 9. The Fix Is In

t's Super Bowl LIX (2025). The Seattle Seahawks take to the field, having won the coin toss. Their new rookie starter approaches the ball and gives it a powerful boot. To everyone's amazement, the ball flies perfectly through the air and crosses dead center at the opposing team's goalposts, for the first ever kickoff field goal in NFL history.[1] The crowd goes wild! After two more downs, the Seahawks regain possession of the ball on the fifty-yard line. Instead of the usual scrimmage to run the ball down the field, they attempt another field goal. The ball sails perfectly through the goalposts once again. Three points! And again. And again. The crowd grows restless, because the game isn't proceeding quite as expected. After scoring thirty consecutive field goals without throwing so much as a single pass, the Seahawks take the trophy as the crowd boos them off the field.

Everyone knows that something's gone terribly wrong, but they're not quite sure what. Theories abound that the Seahawks' new kicker has somehow been genetically enhanced; that Jesus has finally returned and he lives in Seattle; that the whole event is some sort of freak statistical accident due to global warming.

It soon emerges the team has fielded the first ever lightweight place-kicking intelligent shoe. It meets all the existing NFL regulations, but it guides the kicker's foot to exactly the optimal position. Freed from having to aim, the player simply swings his leg as hard as he can, and all that energy drives the ball 50 percent further than normal to precisely where it is supposed to go.

A loud and shrill public debate ensues, and people fall into four highly opinionated camps. The conservatives believe in the sanctity of the current rules and regulations. They have worked just fine ever since they can remember and are perfect just as they are. If the teams want to innovate, we shouldn't interfere with their inventive spirit. As long as it's literally a level playing field, and all teams are permitted to develop similar technologies, things are as they should be. If a team can't afford to develop its own intelligent shoe, that's just survival of the fittest, so it's just tough luck.

In fact, conservatives are suspicious that most or all of the rule changes since the NFL was founded in 1920 have only made things worse. They tout several Washington sports-analysis think-tank studies underwritten by a murky network of wealthy ex-players seeking to protect their respective world records from being surpassed due to any changing of the rules. A well-funded public relations campaign by the nonprofit Americans for Freedom of Footwear promotes the slogan "Kick the bureaucrats, not the innovators" in TV ads showing teams stumbling around the field in leg irons. They stage formal "Foot Ball" fund-raisers across the country for affluent donors.

The liberals are focused on fairness. They don't want to prevent progress, but they also don't want to see some teams get an enduring advantage while others perpetually fall further behind. They say the shoes should be allowed, but the opposing goalposts for teams that use them should be automatically narrowed as the game proceeds to keep the number of successful field goals about average.

A loose-knit consortium of PR firms starts a public-interest "IntegRITy" campaign, but no one can quite figure out what RIT is supposed to stand for. An SOS (Save Our Sneakers) benefit concert, featuring familiar do-gooder musical stars, is organized to raise awareness of the problem and collect funds to install the complicated high-tech electronic goalposts in schools and stadiums around the world, but it turns out that no one with less than a master's degree can figure out how to work them. Raising over $100 million, the firms proudly announce that this will cover an estimated .5 percent of all qualified football fields.

The fundamentalists think anything new should be banned. They romanticize a mostly fanciful past, when life was simple and wonderful before it was corrupted by modern influences. The more extreme among them believe that for good measure, all players should be required to play without shoes at all, the way God intended. Leveraging a well-organized network of church groups, the fundamentalists start a "Ban the Boot" campaign. They bus outraged senior citizens to participate in strident protests before each professional football game, urging a public boycott, after which they receive complimentary admission tickets and drink coupons.

The progressives take a different view. They believe that the purpose of the game is to serve the public interest by staging a skill-based contest that entertains a broad audience while inspiring athletes everywhere to do their best. If rules have to occasionally be tweaked in response to new developments to achieve this goal, that's perfectly okay. In fact, that's the primary duty of the NFL's elected officers.

If pressed, sensible conservatives, liberals, and fundamentalists grudgingly agree with the progressives. They may differ on why things got messed up in the first place, but now that they have, something must be done to put the fun back in the game. Their gripe, however, is that the progressives have yet to put forward a workable idea minimally acceptable to everyone, other than investing more in public education to teach high school players how to kick better.

I'm an economic progressive. I don't think we should tinker with things just for the heck of it, but the purpose of our economy is to serve the public interest, rather than the other way around. None of us—rich, poor, diligent, lazy, adventurous, or habitual—wants to live in a world where members of a small cadre of superrich can have anything they want while the masses suffer in silent misery. The engines of prosperity can motor on, driving up statistical benchmarks of aggregate wealth and abundance, but if more people are leading impoverished and unhappy lives, we aren't measuring the right things. The average income can continue to rise, the gross domestic product can grow, the count of Tesla showrooms can double, but if the national pastime is scanning job boards for supplemental part-time work, we're moving in the wrong direction.

Several economic studies have found that the overall self-reported level of happiness is highest when the economic disparities in society are minimized, even after controlling for all other known factors.[2] In particular, the range of incomes is more strongly correlated with lower satisfaction than the overall level of wealth after a certain minimal wealth threshold is exceeded. If you're skeptical, consider that the average income and percentage of the population working in agriculture in the United States in 1800, adjusted for inflation, were about the same as those in modern-day Mozambique and Uganda.[3] I doubt that most people in Thomas Jefferson's time thought of themselves as wretchedly poor.

Several prominent academics have spent their careers documenting the increasing disparities of income and wealth in the United States and studying their causes, so I won't regale you with statistics here.[4] The short story is that since the end of World War II the country's economy has grown fairly steadily, with a few blips (most notably in the past fifteen years). Before about 1970, these gains were shared equitably between rich and poor. Since that time, however, nearly all the gains have gone to the rich, leaving the poor behind.

A brief analogy may be helpful to get a feel for the nature and scope of this shift as well as its consequences.[5] Imagine a town with one hundred families whose primary source of income is 1,000 acres of orchards. In 1970, the five wealthiest families owned an average of 30 acres of fruit trees each, while the twenty poorest families owned only 3 acres each—quite a spread. A visitor to the town would see a typical assortment of establishments in the town center, such as a diner, shoe store, and haberdashery.

By 2010, an additional 800 acres had been added to the town's productive farmland—a remarkable 80 percent increase in total wealth. But the wealthiest five families now owned an average of 70 acres of fruit trees each—more than twice as many—while the poorest twenty families still owned only 3 acres each. The peculiar thing is that while the average family now farms 18 acres, up from 10 in 1970, fully half the town is struggling to survive on less than 8 acres. More conspicuously, the richest family in town now owns 360 acres, or 20 percent of all the town's productive farmland. In short, the additional land went disproportionately to the already rich, to the point where the less fortunate half of the town got little to nothing.

A visitor returning to the town after a forty-year absence observes a remarkable transformation. Once a humdrum collection of workaday stores, it now sports upscale establishments with the latest luxury goods. The town diner has gone out of business because far fewer people could afford to eat out, and in its place stands a gourmet restaurant, frequented almost exclusively by the wealthiest twenty families in town. The shop windows that used to display galoshes now showcase designer pumps, and the haberdashery has become an haute couture boutique. What beautiful improvements— the townspeople must be so pleased! Unfortunately, what the visitor can't see is that most of the residents never visit these stores. Instead they drive to a Walmart fifty miles away to pick up in bulk the weekly staples they can afford.

Enormous disparities in living standards are a public disgrace, and we need to fix it.

I'm old enough to remember when being rich meant that you had a color TV, and being poor meant you could afford only a black-and-white set. Other than that, people mostly went to the same (public) schools, ate at the same restaurants, and waited in the same lines at Disneyland. But not even the Magic Kingdom can defy economic realities. As far as I can determine, the VIP Tour option for Disneyland was added around 2010. For an additional $315–$380 *per hour,* you get your own guide and unlimited access to Fastpass lines. A rather poignant comment posted on InsideTheMagic.net reads: "Walt Disney never wanted his park(s) to be for rich people only. . . . I dream of a day when ordinary people can once again walk right down the middle of Main Street U.S.A. When kids, rich and poor, can get a hug from Mickey or a kiss from a princess."

To address the scourge of increasing economic inequality, it's helpful to set a goal. You can pick your favorite, but mine is to target a distribution of income roughly like that of 1970, when the top 5 percent of households brought home about ten times as much, on average, as the bottom 20 percent, as opposed to the twenty times we see today. Not great, but close enough for government work. I'm not at all advocating that we return to the economic and social policies of that age, which arguably weren't really helping even back then. Marginal tax rates were way too high, racial inequality was rampant, water and air were far more polluted than they are today (at least in the United States), and tobacco companies promoted their products to children.[6]

Recent American history is full of examples of the government establishing a high-level goal in the interest of promoting social welfare, putting some sensible policies in place, and making it happen. One ongoing example is the push to encourage homeownership in the United States. Studies over time, not to mention common sense, suggest that communities where people own their own homes are safer, more stable, and attractive to investment.[7] As far back as 1918, when the U.S. Department of Labor started a campaign called Own Your Own Home, federal and state governments have promoted this goal with tax policies, regulation of financial institutions, and direct support for homeowners.[8]

As President Johnson said in his proposal to create the Department of Housing and Urban Development (HUD) in 1968, "Homeownership is a cherished dream and achievement of most Americans. But it has always been out of reach of the nation's low-income families. Owning a home can increase responsibility and stake out a man's place in his community. The man who owns a home has something to be proud of and good reason to protect and preserve it."[9]

The motivations for the numerous housing initiatives in support of this lofty goal are mixed, to say the least. Many of these programs had surreptitious objectives such as subsidizing the housing industry, creating construction jobs or, most remarkably, enshrining segregation.[10] Nonetheless, the country got the job done. From 1900 to today, homeownership increased by 40 percent, so that owners occupy nearly two out of every three homes.[11]

Another area with considerable success has been the reduction of air and water pollution in the United States. Since the Environmental Protection Agency (EPA) was founded in 1970, aggregate measures of major air pollutants (with the notable exception of carbon dioxide, not classified as such until 2009) have been reduced by a remarkable 68 percent, even though the GDP has increased by 65 percent.[12] Growing up in New York City in the mid-1960s, I thought the natural color of the afternoon sky was a brownish orange, and the conventional wisdom back then was that living in the nation's largest city was equivalent to smoking two packs of cigarettes a day. (Which, incidentally, wasn't considered a significant health risk.)

Most of this improvement was due to regulation of polluters (mainly by levying fines), standards for equipment manufacturers (such as vehicles), and technological advances. More recently, emissions trading, better known as cap and trade, has begun to gain traction. This is a much more flexible and rational approach because it uses market forces to allocate resources efficiently, replacing a crude system of hodgepodge rules and central controls. Water quality is more complex because of the different measures of purity, but in general it shows similar improvements.

In the financial domain, the United States has a long-standing goal of easing the lot of the elderly. It used to be that, for most people, getting old meant living in squalor. As soon as your useful working life ended, you were in dire financial straits.[13] This no doubt contributed significantly to premature death. But easing our elders' suffering is more than altruism—that could be you in a few years, if you're lucky enough to live that long. Our Social Security system, adopted shortly after the Great Depression in 1935, and low-cost or free medical care (Medicare and Medicaid) were major steps forward in addressing this problem. In addition to these mandatory public savings programs, there are a myriad of U.S. government policies that encourage saving for retirement by sequestering assets into personal accounts, such as individual retirement accounts (IRAs).

But the biggest win has been in public health. Here the measure is clear and personal: a male born in the United States in 1850 could expect to live on average to be about thirty-eight years old; one born in 2000 can expect to live to about seventy-five years old—whatever that means, because he would only be fifteen years old today. (Much of the increase resulted from a reduction of infant mortality.)[14] As my nonagenarian mother proudly remarks, ninety is the new seventy!

The rise in life expectancy is due to many factors but is largely the result of improvements in medical sanitation, the development of vaccines, public efforts to separate water and sewer systems, government initiatives such as the creation of the Centers for Disease Control, and public health education campaigns (smoking cessation, for example).

So the time has arrived for us to establish sensible policies to reduce income inequality. Our initial instinct may be to tackle this challenge by first determining its root cause(s) and addressing each in turn, most notably unemployment. But I suspect that would simply embroil us in endless debates, pitting those who blame the poor for their own failure to thrive against those who blame needless government spending and regulatory interference against those who see those same regulations as hopelessly biased toward the rich against those who believe your income is a numerical measure of how pleased God is with you.

Some would likely argue we should raise taxes and spend more on social programs. Others would counter that this will impede the "entrepreneurial spirit" by reducing the rewards for risk taking and hard work.[15] Some would point the finger at layabout welfare recipients. Occupy Wall Streeters might take a similarly dim view of the investment bankers of Goldman Sachs, which *Rolling Stone* famously referred to as a "great vampire squid wrapped around the face of humanity, relentlessly jamming its blood funnel into anything that smells like money."[16] Perhaps a new federal jobs program is the ticket, reprising Franklin Delano Roosevelt's WPA program, which employed almost 8 million people.[17]

But I propose that these approaches conflate two things we should consider separately: jobs and income. Jobs may be scarcer in the future, but that doesn't mean that income has to be. Everyone needs an income to live, and the most obvious way to get one is to work for money. So most proposed solutions revolve around ensuring that everyone has an opportunity to earn a decent wage for an honest day's work, or at least to give people something to tide them over while they try to find one. But it's not the only way.

In fact, there are two groups of people without jobs. The first are those who are looking for a job and can't find one. Indeed, that's the official U.S. Bureau of Labor Statistics definition of being unemployed. The other group is what the bureau calls "not in the labor force," which includes retirees. This doesn't mean these people aren't working, just that they aren't getting paid for working. (Me, for instance. I was quoted in the *New York Times* in 2003 as quipping "I used to be retired, . . . now I'm just unemployed.")[18] I'd like to think

I'm a productive member of society, making a contribution, but I'm not collecting a paycheck, which is fine by me.

We tend to cast a skeptical eye on the jobless—unless they have a lot of money. Then it's okay—indeed, it's often celebrated. No one expects Paris Hilton to be anything other than an idle rich girl, an image that she has polished to a high art, despite a dizzying array of gigs, product endorsements, TV and movie appearances, and recording contracts, earning her an estimated $6.5 million in 2005 alone.[19]

You don't have to have a fortune to live off your assets. It all depends on how you want to live. Just how much is enough?

For years, pundits have lamented that the median household income in the United States has stagnated even as productivity and total income have been rising relentlessly.[20] On the surface, this is an argument about increasing income inequality, but it glosses over an important detail: how does the average family feel about that? If people had the opportunity to work more and make more money, would they? Or are they satisfied with their work/life balance as it is?

Here are some facts that suggest many people aren't working more simply because they don't need to or want to. Starting with the long-term historical trend, you might be surprised to learn that in the nineteenth century, most people worked about sixty to seventy hours a week.[21] They had virtually no free time at all. In 1791, carpenters in Philadelphia actually went on strike to demand a reduction in hours to a ten-hour workday.[22] The federal government first got involved in 1916 with the Adamson Act, which set the standard workday as eight hours, but only for railroad workers. By 1937, this shortened workday became part of the Fair Labor Standards Act.[23] While this trend toward fewer working hours is continuing through today, it's quite gradual. Federal Reserve data from 1950 to 2011 shows an

11 percent reduction in total hours worked per year.[24] Today, contrary to public perception, the average working person puts in about thirty-four hours of paid labor a week.[25]

In contrast to working hours, real wages and incomes have soared. To pick a single example, U.S. males employed full-time year-round have seen their inflation-adjusted average incomes just short of double since 1955. Working women have seen their incomes soar more than that, by 138 percent. Full-time employed people literally have twice as much money to spend after inflation.[26]

But this story gets really interesting when you look at it on a household basis. According to the U.S. Census Bureau, the median household income in 1995 was $51,719. By 2012, it was virtually unchanged, at $51,758.[27] (The 1995 figure is adjusted for inflation.) However, the median net wage of a U.S. worker (inflation adjusted) rose approximately 14 percent during the same period. (The nominal increase was 65 percent less the cumulate inflation rate of 51 percent.)[28] So what could account for this discrepancy? Households don't work—people do. And the number of adults working in the average household dropped 8 percent during that period, from 1.36 to 1.25.[29]

The number of working adults in a household is affected by a number of factors. Unemployment in 2012 was 2.5 percent higher than in 1995. This is a little tricky to calculate, but the average number of working-age adults in households dropped by about 2.5 percent.[30] That's no doubt part of the story, but what's the rest? At least one plausible explanation is that people are making more money when they work, so when those benefits are shared (that is, in households), many couples (related or not) simply decide to work less in total.

Whether people make this decision because it's too much of a hassle to look for more work or a better job or because they just prefer to spend their time doing other things is really just two sides of the same coin. Their decision to find work or to do something else with their time is a rational decision based on the vagaries of their local labor market and how they prefer to live.[31] Consider the example of my former employee Emmie Nastor. His biggest objection to his job was not the pay but the (compulsory) hours. He would gladly accept less pay if it means he can reliably get home before his newborn son goes to bed.

So where does the tacit assumption come from that every able-bodied, red-blooded American who can work is going to do so as much as he or she possibly can? It's a reflection of a skewed concept of progress, or at least wishful thinking, that is baked into our government policies. Many people believe that our legislators tax, borrow, and spend more than they should. I have no informed opinion on this. But the historical way we have addressed our economic problems is to grow our way out of them. What looks like a mountain of national debt today will seem far less daunting when the bill comes due if only we can continue to expand our economy each year. If it still proves to be a problem, we can fall back on adjusting the inflation rate by expanding the money supply, so the cost of repayment is more manageable. The government uses this same logic when it supports retired Social Security recipients with receipts from current workers. (Which will shortly become a problem because the relevant population of workers is trending down relative to the population of retirees for the moment.)

This can-do attitude of bigger-faster-stronger is so deeply ingrained in our American mind-set that benchmarks of countervailing beliefs are difficult to find. When a parent decides to stay home and take care of the kids, he or she falls off the government's measures of economic value. When someone quits his or her job as a real estate agent to play guitar in a rock band, disposable income may go down even as personal satisfaction goes up.

This is not to say that those with the smallest incomes would make the same decisions. Living from paycheck to paycheck, or on no paycheck at all, is certainly no picnic. But those in the storied middle class may not be as anxious as we might assume to climb to the next level, if the price is their free time and satisfaction with their job.

But this time-tested government principle—that we can grow our way out of our economic problems—offers a practical approach to reducing income inequality. We don't need to take anything away from anyone, we simply need to distribute future growth in a more equitable way and the problem will take care of itself.

To understand how this can work, let's start with a simple hypothetical. Suppose everyone were to magically retire today. Just what would everyone's household income be? First we need to look at how wealthy the people in the United States really are, on average. Combining data from the Federal Reserve and the Census Bureau for 2012, the average U.S. household has a net worth of approximately $600,000 for its 2.6 residents.[32] That includes bank accounts, stocks and bonds, private retirement funds, and real estate, after subtracting all debt. It excludes nonproductive assets like cars, furnishings, and personal possessions. But that doesn't count Social Security. Total Social Security trust fund assets were $3 trillion at the end of 2013,[33] which adds about another $25,000, for a grand total of $625,000 per household.

How much retirement income would this generate? The S&P

500, a reasonable proxy for the U.S. equity markets, provided an annual return of more than 11 percent for the past fifty years, while ten-year U.S. Treasury bills, considered one of the safest investments in the world, averaged nearly 7 percent.[34] Assuming you held half of a portfolio in stocks and half in bonds, the average return would have been around 9 percent per year. If you wanted to reserve enough money in this portfolio to compensate for the historical rate of inflation (3 percent), you could spend about 6 percent annually. (Not accounting for capital gains taxes, if any. If this doesn't match your current mileage, note that the inflation rate and typical investment returns, at least for bonds, are well below the historical ranges at the moment.)

Applying 6 percent to the aggregate U.S. wealth, each household could spend about $40,000 per year and still keep up with inflation. That's *in addition* to whatever the household might (optionally) earn, and it assumes that people leave their entire estate intact to their heirs when they die rather than spending it themselves, giving those in the next generation an enormous head start on their own retirement. (Except for any estate taxes, of course, which you wouldn't owe if you died today with $625,000 in assets in the United States because of the lifetime exemption.) In fact, if the population is not growing or it were shrinking (as it is in much of Europe), members of the next generation wouldn't need to add to this portfolio, which is to say they might never need to work at all.

Another way to arrive at these figures is to look at how the financial markets value all public companies and bonds. At the end of 2011, the value of the U.S. bond market was just under $37 trillion, with U.S. stocks at $21 trillion, for a total of $58 trillion.[35] But only about two-thirds of that is owned domestically, so let's use $39 trillion. (Contrary to popular perception, China owns only about 8 percent of the national debt.)[36] Adding the $25 trillion of value stored in homes and subtracting mortgage debt of $13 trillion, that works out to $51 trillion, or about $450,000 per household.[37] But that doesn't include the value of all privately held companies, or loans to companies and individuals, which probably accounts for a portion of the difference between this estimate and the $625,000 above.

That's now, but let's talk about the future. Data for the last thirty years shows a GDP growth rate per person, after inflation, of approximately 1.6 percent.[38] Assuming this trend is to continue, the total increase in real wealth per person in forty years would be 90 percent. That is to say, the average person in the United States will be almost twice as wealthy in forty years as today, based on current trends. This is consistent with the 80 percent growth experienced in the past forty years, as I noted earlier. And as you might expect from the previous chapters, I think this is a gross underestimate— but that's just one person's opinion. This equates to an annual household income, purely from investments, of about $75,000 in today's dollars. Not bad.

But surely this rosy picture can't be right. People are struggling. Most people are losing ground. It's a bloodbath out there. It surely doesn't feel like most people are earning $40,000 just sitting around doing nothing. All correct—for the simple reason that the distribution of assets isn't broad enough. These averages don't mean anything right now because the wealth isn't owned equitably by all households—the precise problem we're looking to address. But we don't need to redistribute today's wealth to make a serious dent in the problem of income inequality—that ship has already sailed. Instead, we can focus on new ways to distribute future gains. But how?

We can put in place economic incentives to broaden the ownership base for stocks and bonds. The incentives are not for the owners themselves but for the corporations and issuers of the bonds. We can put their self-interests to work for the rest of us, as we do in other aspects of our capitalist economy.

To date, the U.S. government grants most tax policies and economic incentives (often called "loopholes") to encourage corporations to make certain types of investments, or to reduce the cost of borrowing money (as in the case of tax-free municipal bonds). These same techniques can be used to spread the future ownership of the assets necessary to support retirement or reduced work.

To understand how this works, consider two hypothetical future corporations in the same business: operating online superstores that sell groceries to consumers with guaranteed delivery within three hours, regardless of location: "My Mart" and "People's Provisions." Both are run by talented and well-compensated management teams, but My Mart is owned by the ten superrich heirs of the recently deceased baron of industry Marty Martin, while People's Provisions' publicly traded shares are owned directly or indirectly by 100 million people.

Both companies have made tremendous investments in automation, reducing their workforces to the bare minimum possible with current technology. They have become so efficient that the revenue per employee is in the tens of millions of dollars. For comparison, Walmart, one of the most efficient retail companies in the world, generated $213,000 in revenue per employee in 2013. Both companies are extremely profitable, delivering nearly $100 billion in annual profits, compared to Walmart's $17 billion today. For My Mart, that works out to nearly $10 billion a year for each of the lucky heirs. But its rival People's Provisions is sending dividend checks each year for $1,000 to nearly one-third of the U.S. population.

Now, which company is better serving the public interest? Both are doing a terrific job of delivering goods and services to their customers, and both are highly motivated to continue to improve so they can increase their market share. But People's Provisions is also serving the financial interests of a significant fraction of the public, as opposed to a single family of playboys and patrons of the arts. In that sense, it's delivering far more benefit to society.

Before we can address this inequity, we need an objective way to measure it. One thing the federal government does well is collect and publish statistics. Sometimes this is used to inform policy, but other times it's intended to make us better consumers by giving us the information we need to make good decisions. For instance, the Energy Star program places EnergyGuide stickers on all sorts of consumer products, such as washers, refrigerators, and televisions, with standardized measures of energy consumption and operating costs.[39] By law, the window stickers on new cars must show the EPA fuel-economy ratings and NHTSA (National Highway Traffic Safety Administration) crash-test rating. In the financial sphere, the relative risks of corporate and government bonds are rated by three well-respected private services (Moody's, Standard & Poor's, and Fitch Ratings). Institutional Shareholder Services (ISS) issues a widely used measure of corporate governance covering board structure, shareholder rights, compensation practices, and audit quality.

What we need to lay the groundwork for addressing income inequality is a new government measure of just how broadly assets are owned. Luckily, we can take one off the shelf, dust it off, and polish it up a bit.

In 1912, an Italian statistician named Corrado Gini published a paper titled "Variabilità e mutabilità" or, in English, "Variability and Mutability."[40] In it, he proposed a clever measure of dispersion which has come to be known as the Gini coefficient. Basically, you feed in a bunch of data, and the Gini coefficient will tell you just how "even" the series is, expressed as 0 for smooth and equal, and 1 for incredibly skewed. It can be applied to lots of different situations, but its most common current use is to measure economic data of just the sort we are concerned with here. For instance, the U.S. Census Bureau uses it to measure income inequality.[41] In 1970, the Gini coefficient for income stood at .394. By 2011, it had climbed to .477. That doesn't have an intuitive ring to it, but it's pretty bad.

The same objective measure can be applied to the beneficial ownership of any asset. Suppose you and three friends decide to go in together on a rental property. If you each have one-quarter ownership, that's a Gini coefficient of 0. On the other hand, suppose you put up all the money but decide to cut in your friends for 1 percent each because you're a nice person. That's a Gini coefficient close to 1. But suppose that the arrangement doesn't work out because your friends act like they own the place, when for all practical purposes you do. So you buy out their interests. The Gini coefficient goes back to 0, because all the owners (that is, just you) have equal shares.

As you can see, just applying the Gini coefficient to an asset doesn't get at what we want to measure. Instead, we have to make a small adjustment. First we need to define some population, say, adult U.S. citizens. Then assume for calculation purposes that people in the group who don't own any of the assets have a 0 percent interest. Now the Gini coefficient reflects how widely owned the asset is across the population of interest. We could name such an index, applied to individual assets such as a stock or bond, the public benefit index, or PBI. For ease of use, let's subtract it from 1, multiply it by 100, and round it to the nearest integer—in other words, make the PBI scale from 0 to 100, where 100 means very equitable, and 0 is highly concentrated.

Consider the PBI for the two hypothetical corporations described above. Even though the patriarch Marty Martin's ten super-wealthy heirs have equal shares of his fortune, when you count in everyone else, the PBI would be close to 0. However, the more widely held Public Provisions might have a PBI closer to 30.

In a sense, public government-owned assets like national parks, which are available for use by everyone, have a PBI of 100. However, Michael Jackson's Neverland Ranch, which he built almost entirely for his own amusement, would have a PBI of 0.

The PBI, as defined here, isn't perfect. For example, it may be complex to compute it for the beneficial owners (as opposed to the nominal owners).[42] But it's probably adequate for the purposes of this discussion.

Now we can get to the meat of the problem. We've established a goal (income distribution approximately that of 1970), and we've got an objective measure of the public utility of a financial asset (its PBI). But this is just a number we can slap on stocks and bonds like the window sticker on a new car. How do we use it to reduce wealth and income inequality?

Let's start with corporate tax policies. Some studies suggest that reducing or eliminating all corporate taxes would increase overall wealth.[43] The problem, of course, is that this would mostly or exclusively make the stockholders more wealthy, not the general public. But suppose you were to scale taxes, or give tax breaks, to corporations with high PBI scores. This would put the more broadly owned companies at a competitive advantage. They could afford to invest more and ultimately expand their market (and market value), at the expense of more closely held competitors.

For our hypothetical online groceries, suppose that People's Provisions had an effective corporate tax rate of 15 percent, while My Mart paid the (current) maximum of 35 percent. That would mean that People's Provisions could afford to put $20 billion more to work than My Mart each year. It could build more distribution centers, offer better service, advertise widely, reduce prices, and increase dividends. Over time, its market share would grow, while My Mart's share would shrink, generating more profits that would be distributed to an ever-widening swath of society.

Now, how would the stockholders of My Mart be likely to react? After reluctantly accepting the fact that their highly paid army of lobbyists isn't able to get this tax policy reversed in their favor, they would have a simple decision to make—or, more accurately, to instruct their accountants to make. They might just keep collecting their enormous after-tax profits, but they might be better off selling part of their interest to the public, in order to raise My Mart's PBI and therefore lower its tax rate, increasing their profits while making the company more competitive.

But People's Provisions isn't standing still. Seeing the significant benefits conferred by its broad ownership, it undertakes an investor relations campaign to expand it even further. The company makes a secondary offering of stock, with a twist. Taking a page from its own sales promotions, it agrees to pay the brokerage commissions for any shares sold to a new stockholder, effectively giving the new owners a discount for a "first-time purchase," and requires that the stock be held for some prescribed period of time, say, five years. It also offers an incentive bonus to its underwriters' legion of retail stockbrokers for hawking the offering to new stockholders. This offering is so successful that its entire cost is covered by the first three years' reduction in corporate tax.

Not to be outdone, My Mart responds with a unique promotion: for every $500 a customer spends with the company, it offers a 50 percent discount from the current market price on the purchase of up to ten newly issued My Mart shares to qualified buyers. Each time you shop, you accumulate My Mart Points that you can cash in for stock.

In short, companies subject to this sort of tax incentive will find ways to distribute the ownership of their stock more broadly in order to reap the tax advantages. Even better, the government can monitor and adjust this process by changing how corporate taxes vary in response to the PBI. Similar incentives can apply to the issuance of bonds, though that's a bit more complex. So, is the problem solved?

Not quite yet. That sounds great, but where are people with no assets going to get the money to buy securities in the first place?

There are lots of ways to address this, and to suggest just one, we could change the way we manage Social Security. Instead of relying on a monolithic and opaque centralized system of investment, we could give individuals more visibility and control over their own vested balances. We could permit people to select from a basket of individual stocks and bonds, or stock and bond funds, to tailor their portfolio as they wish, within certain bounds. This is similar to the way private retirement funds like 401K plans currently operate.

This has several advantages. First, it allows a much broader pool of people to play an active role in managing their retirement funds. By providing both higher visibility and at least a modicum of personal control, it enhances the sense of personal connection to society—a feeling that you, too, are participating in the American dream. Rather than the government simply taking money out of your paycheck with the distant promise that you may or may not get it back if you retire someday, you will understand where it's going, what it's worth, and how much you are going to get when the time comes. It's harder to smash the display windows of a store in East Los Angeles when you are holding its stock in your Social Security account, without feeling that you are in part hurting yourself.

This additional visibility can also address a problem that currently bedevils the Social Security trust funds. Since none of us really has any idea how much of our money the government is investing on our behalf, it's difficult for politicians to adjust the benefits paid to the actual rate of investment return and demographic trends. This is why changes to Social Security benefits are sometimes called the "third rail" of U.S. politics. But if people can see that the value of their portfolio went up or down this year, and their ultimate payments are tied to it, the whole system will not only make more sense, it can eliminate the need for legislative adjustments altogether. No more unfunded mandates, as is currently the case with our Social Security system.

But this isn't the only way to get the ball rolling. Negative income taxes, government grants and rebates, and matching funds for various activities we want to encourage can help build each citizen's portfolio. Rather than wait for someone to get a job before starting a Social Security account, the government could offer to add high-PBI stocks and bonds to the portfolio of people who volunteer for public-service work such as caring for the elderly, cleaning up parks, counseling troubled teens, distributing health education pamphlets, and the like. This could apply to retirees as well as those idled through unemployment or those who simply have some free time to spare.

To encourage commitment and continuity, the government could take a page out of the Silicon Valley startup playbook: restricted stock vesting. You sign up for some public-service activity and are granted a pool of shares that you don't actually own yet. As you work, these shares become yours (vest) over time. This way, you are always cognizant of the consequences of quitting prematurely, and you have a goal and scorecard with which to monitor your progress.

The idea that everyone is a stockholder in society and has a retirement account automatically opened for them (say) on their tenth birthday would alter the sense of integration and participation in society. It would encourage public service and help people feel productive even if they aren't directly earning a paycheck.

But the line between preretirement and postretirement needn't be quite as sharp as it is today. As our cumulative wealth continues to grow, it will become more reasonable to permit people to receive dividend payments earlier than their golden years. In other words, we can allow working-age people to draw partial benefits and also reduce the full-benefit retirement age. In the extreme, your Social Security account, in conjunction with more garden-variety retirement and savings accounts, may provide substantial financial support throughout your working life.

Which brings us back to jobs. Money is not the only reason to work. People like to feel that they are useful members of society.

They enjoy making a contribution to the welfare of others in addition to providing for themselves and their families. Most people feel great satisfaction in helping others, increasing their sense of self-worth, and giving their lives purpose and meaning.

In the future, some may decide to sit around all day playing video games if they have sufficient income to support themselves without working. But most people won't settle for that. They won't want to remain on the bottom rung of society, no matter how comfortable that rung may be in real terms. Some will still want to work at bona fide paying jobs, if for no other reason than to increase their standard of living, social status, and attractiveness to a mate. These instincts aren't going to go away. But for others, a regular job may be seen as something of a cop-out, a self-centered way to get more for yourself without giving much back. They may choose to work part-time, or not at all, and instead to volunteer for government-certified public-service projects that will further enhance their retirement nest egg.

People aren't only going to fish and golf full-time. They will also learn to play piano, paint, write poetry, grow prize orchids, sell handmade arts and crafts, care for wounded animals, exercise, and homeschool their kids. All these things are more than hobbies; they deliver real benefits to society.

The key to dealing with a shrinking pool of available jobs is not to create artificial ones by government fiat. It's to rebalance the supply of economically motivated workers with the available pool of paid jobs. We can do this by adjusting the incentives for people to do other productive things with their time.

I'm by no means the first one to consider what the world will be like when our basic needs can be met without our own labor.

None other than John Maynard Keynes, the legendary economist, wrote a fascinating meditation on this question in 1930 entitled "Economic Possibilities for Our Grandchildren." In this thoughtful essay, he projects that within a century (which is nearly up, of course), continued economic growth would permit us to meet the basic needs of all humans with little to no effort. As he puts it, "All this means in the long run *that mankind is solving its economic problem*" (his italics). He goes on to distinguish between absolute needs and relative needs, suggesting that once the former are met, many people will "devote their energies to non-economic purposes."[44] His economic analysis was spot on but, to our disgrace, his expectations for wealth distribution have yet to be realized.

As we transition to a world where most of the work currently requiring human effort and attention succumbs to automation, it's essential to distribute the benefits of our increased wealth beyond those who land the remaining good jobs or are lucky enough to accumulate private assets. Ultimately, we may find ourselves living in a symbiotic or possibly parasitic relationship with the machines, as I will explain shortly.

So what about Super Bowl LIX and the problem of the intelligent place-kicking shoe? After much deliberation, the NFL hit upon a creative solution. It established an annual $1 million prize for the best improvements in players' gear, with carefully proscribed limits as to what contestants could and could not do. The resulting inventions were made freely available to all teams in the league.

Soon, innovations were everywhere, some of which necessitated changes to the rules of the game. Most notably, some clever MIT engineering students developed a shoe that allowed players to jump impossibly high in the air and land safely on their feet. With this new footwear, it became increasingly hard to kick a field goal because the opposing team's players could simply jump high enough to intercept the ball. Professional football games started to feel like the quidditch competitions of Harry Potter fame, in which players fly through the air on magic broomsticks. So the NFL added a height restriction on the games. A ball flying over forty feet in the air was out of bounds, and any player whose helmet crossed a height of thirty feet was automatically offside.

Not only did this restore the fun of the sport, but attendance and revenues were higher than ever as the players developed a whole new class of breathtaking athletic moves. The NFL commissioner, in his annual remarks, described the new gear as the greatest improvement to football since the instant replay.

Still, some people were unhappy with these developments. They preferred the old-fashioned game in which players wore uniforms and gear made only of ordinary materials. So they formed a new league, the CFL (Classic Football League), which became quite popular among a certain set of old-timers and purists.

Problem solved.

# Welcome to Your Children's Future

erhaps this pontificating pundit can pass on some pithy prognostications about our prospects? (May I offer some speculation about our future?)

Words matter. How we say things colors what we think. Words describe, capture, and communicate, but they also frame our understanding and shape our imagination. We naturally interpret new experiences in terms of old, and which experiences we choose as reference points alters how we see our world.

In the preceding chapters, I've described how the nature of work shifts in response to the introduction of innovative technologies, though this shift may lag their deployment considerably. The same is true of language. It shifts in response to changes in the things that we need to reason and communicate about. And, like the labor markets, our language doesn't always keep up with the consequences of advancing technology. Sometimes our words don't fit; other times the concepts are so new that appropriate terms simply don't yet exist. And that's a problem. It's hard to understand what's happening, much less formulate appropriate plans and policies, if you can't talk about it.

Language adapts to meet our needs in interesting ways. Sometimes we simply invent new words, like *outroduction, wackadoodle, cra-cra, trick out,* and *fantabulous.* Sometimes we jam two words together and fuse their meanings, like *brunch* (breakfast plus lunch), *smog* (smoke plus fog), *motel* (motor plus hotel).[1] But most of the time, we awkwardly employ old words for new purposes, gritting our teeth until the expanded or changed meaning becomes commonplace.

One of my favorite examples of our language adapting to technological advancement is the meaning of the word *music*. The phonograph was invented in 1877 by Thomas Edison and improved by Alexander Graham Bell in the 1880s with his use of wax cylinders as a recording medium. Before that time, if you wanted to hear music, the only way to do it was to listen to someone perform it. There was simply no notion of separating the act of production from the sound produced, and so there was no need to consider whether actually making the music was essential to the concept.

So how did people react upon hearing the first recorded music? Consider the harsh reaction of John Philip Sousa, composer of many familiar military marches (such as "The Stars and Stripes Forever"). In reaction to the emergence of recording devices, Sousa wrote a diatribe in 1906 entitled "The Menace of Mechanical Music." He said, "But heretofore, the whole course of music, from its first day to this, has been along the line of making it the expression of soul states; in other words, of pouring into it soul. . . . The nightingale's song is delightful because the nightingale herself gives it forth. . . . The host of mechanical reproducing machines, in their mad desire to supply music for all occasions, are offering to supplant the . . . dance orchestra. . . . Evidently they believe no field too large for their incursions, no claim too extravagant." He concluded, "Music teaches all that is beautiful in this world. Let us not hamper it with a machine that tells the story day by day, without variation, without soul, barren of the joy, the passion, the ardor that is the inheritance of man alone."[2] In other words, to Sousa, real music required the creative act of a person expressing authentic feelings. In this sense, a machine couldn't make music—the noise emanating from it wasn't the same thing. Even if it sounded similar, it lacked the emotional force necessary to qualify as real "music."

Needless to say, anyone taking this position today would be considered wackadoodle. How silly of Mr. Sousa. Obviously, music is music, regardless of how it's made.

But this argument reprised itself much more recently. When digital (as opposed to analog) recording first emerged, it encountered significant pushback from audiophiles. There was a serious line of thought that something was lost, that some "soul" goes out of music when you represent it in digital form. Many people believed that digital music inevitably sounded flat, lacking the depth and subtlety of analog music. For example, Harry Pearson, founder of the magazine *The Absolute Sound* in 1973, followed in Sousa's footsteps (probably unknowingly) by proclaiming that "LPs [vinyl records] are decisively more musical. CDs drain the soul from music. The emotional involvement disappears." This sentiment was not uncommon among audiophiles. Michael Fremer, editor of the *Tracking Angle* (a music review magazine) was quoted as recently as 1997 saying, "Digital preserves music the way formaldehyde preserves frogs: it kills it and makes it last forever."[3]

Needless to say, anyone taking this position today would be considered cra-cra. How silly of Mr. Pearson and Mr. Fremer. Obviously, music is music, regardless of how it's stored. So our modern concept of "music" includes not only analog recordings, which Sousa rejected, but also digital ones, which Pearson and Fremer rejected. Same word, expanded meaning.

But before we dismiss all these gentlemen as prisoners of their own dated and unenlightened perspectives, consider how you might feel if, in the future, your children ask a computer to play some "Michael Jackson," and instead of reproducing one of the "king of pop's" actual recordings, it instantly composes and synthesizes a series of tracks indistinguishable from his own works by anyone not intimately familiar with his actual oeuvre, including his unique vocal style. Would you feel that this artificial creation is not real "music," and certainly not real "Michael Jackson," because it didn't originate in any sense from a human artist, not to mention the master himself? (Why would anyone tolerate this? To save on the royalties, of course. It wouldn't violate his copyrights.)

You might be tempted to regard this discussion about the meaning of the word *music* as useless pedantry, but that would be misguided. The words we use make a very real and serious impact on how we think and act.

Consider, for example, autonomous vehicles, a.k.a. self-driving cars. When automobiles were first introduced in the early 1900s, people called them "horseless carriages" because the horse-drawn carriage was the nearest reference point with which to grasp the concept of the newfangled machines. (And how many people today realize that "horsepower" actually refers to real horse power?) Now we talk about "driverless cars" for the same reasons. Both phrases are examples of describing new technologies in terms of old, but in doing so, the words obscure their real potential. A "driverless car" sounds like some terrific new technology with which to trick out your next vehicle—like parking sensors or a backup camera. It's just like your old car, except that now you don't have to drive it yourself. But the truth is that this new technology is going to dramatically change the way we think about transportation, with an impact on society far greater than these words suggest. A better description would be "personal public transit."

Why public? Once this technology becomes commonplace, there will be precious little reason to own a car at all. When you need one, you will simply call for it as you might for a taxi today, but it will appear much more reliably and promptly. (Most studies assume that the average wait in metropolitan areas would be around one to two minutes, including peak times.) When you disembark, it will quietly decamp to the nearest staging area to await a call from its next passenger. Within a few decades, you will no more consider purchasing your own car than you would think today of buying a private railroad coach.[4]

The economic, social, and environmental consequences are difficult to overstate. Studies project that traffic accidents will fall by 90 percent. That would save in human lives the equivalent of ten 9/11 attacks annually in the United States alone. Vehicle accidents cause an additional 4 million injuries annually costing over $870 billion annually in the U.S. alone.[5] Then there's the concomitant savings in traffic law enforcement (cops on the road), wrecked cars, vehicle repairs, and traffic courts. Not to mention we will need only one vehicle for every three currently in use.[6] And we're not talking centuries from now; the expert consensus is that 75 percent of the vehicles on the road will be self-driving in twenty to twenty-five years.

This single innovation will transform the way we live. Garages will go the way of outhouses, and countless acres of valuable space wasted on parking lots will be repurposed, essentially manufacturing vast amounts of new real estate.[7] Environmental pollution will be significantly reduced, along with the resultant health effects.

Teens won't suffer the rite-of-passage of learning to drive. Traffic jams will be a quaint memory of more primitive times, not to mention that it may be possible to eliminate speed limits entirely, dramatically reducing commute time. This in turn will expand the distance you can live from your workplace, which will lower real estate costs near cities and raise them further away. Personal productivity will soar because you can do other things in the car besides driving. Auto insurance will become a thing of the past. You can party all night at your local bar without risking your life to get home. The pizza delivery guy will become a mobile vending machine. Fantabulous!

Consider the economic effects of this on the typical family. According to the American Automobile Association (AAA), in 2013 the average car cost the owner $9,151 per year to drive fifteen thousand miles (including depreciation, gas, maintenance, and insurance, but not financing cost). But the average U.S. family has at least two cars,[8] so that's about $18,000 a year. That works out to 60¢ per mile, compared to estimates of 15¢ a mile operating cost for shared autonomous vehicles.[9] So a typical family might see its cost of personal transportation drop by 75 percent, not to mention it will no longer need to pay or borrow all that cash to buy cars in the first place. That's a savings of nearly as much as a family currently spends on food, including eating out.[10] How much extra spending money would you have if all your food were free? According to a 2014 analysis in the *MIT Technology Review*, there's a "potential financial benefit to the U.S. on the order of more than $3 trillion per year."[11] That's an incredible 19 percent of current GDP.

In short, this single application of AI technology changes everything. It alone will make us far richer, safer, and healthier. It will destroy existing jobs (taxi drivers, to name just one) and create new ones (commuter shared club-car concierges, for instance).[12] And there are many, many other coming technologies with potentially comparable impact. That's why I'm supremely confident that our future is very bright—if only we can figure out how to equitably distribute the benefits.

Let's look at another example of language shifting to accommodate new technology, this one predicted by Alan Turing. In 1950 he wrote a thoughtful essay called "Computing Machinery and Intelligence" that opens with the words "I propose to consider the question, 'Can machines think?'" He goes on to define what he calls the "imitation game," what we now know as the Turing Test. In the Turing Test, a computer attempts to fool a human judge into thinking it is human. The judge has to pick the computer out of a lineup of human contestants. All contestants are physically separated from the judges, who communicate with them through text only. Turing speculates, "I believe that in about fifty years' time it will be possible to programme computers . . . to make them play the imitation game so well that an average interrogator will not have more than a 70 per cent chance of making the right identification after five minutes of questioning."[13]

As you might imagine, enthusiastic geeks stage such contests regularly, and by 2008, synthetic intellects were good enough to fool the judges into believing they were human 25 percent of the time.[14] Not bad, considering that most contest entrants were programmed by amateurs in their spare time.

The Turing Test has been widely interpreted as a sort of coming-of-age ritual for AI, a threshold at which machines will have demonstrated intellectual prowess worthy of human respect. But this interpretation of the test is misplaced; it wasn't at all what Turing had in mind. A close reading of his actual paper reveals a different intent: "The original question, 'Can machines think?' I believe to be too meaningless to deserve discussion. Nevertheless I believe that at the end of the century *the use of words and general educated opinion will have altered so much that one will be able to speak of machines thinking without expecting to be contradicted*" (emphasis added).[15]

In other words, Turing wasn't trying to establish a test that machines must pass to join the ranks of the intelligent; he was speculating that by the end of the century the meaning of words like *thinking* and *intelligence* would shift to include any machine that might pass his test, just as the meaning of the word *music* has shifted to accommodate the output of machines that can reproduce the sounds a musician makes. Turing's prediction was not so much about the capabilities of machines as the accepted meaning of words.

It's a little difficult to imagine how you might have reacted back in 1950 if someone referred to a computer going about its business as "thinking," but I strongly suspect it would have been quite jarring, or have seemed like an analogy at best. My guess is that if you traveled back in time with your Apple iPhone to demonstrate Siri, its natural language question-answering module, people would have been unnerved. With human beings as the only relevant touchstones to comprehend this strange golem, they might have seriously questioned whether it was morally acceptable to condemn this apparently sentient being to live a lonely existence confined to a tiny, monolithic slab. Yet today, Apple routinely describes Siri as an "intelligent assistant" without notable objection, and no one in his or her right mind thinks Siri has a mind as well.[16] It also seems perfectly reasonable today to describe IBM's *Jeopardy!*-playing Watson as "thinking" about its answers and exhibiting "intelligence," even though no reasonable person would attribute to it the salient attributes of a human soul, whatever those might be. Though Watson can undoubtedly answer questions about itself in considerable detail, and it clearly monitors its own thought processes, it hardly seems appropriate to call it introspective. Turing deserves full credit—he was obviously quite right.

It's easy to look down our noses at the naïveté of earlier times, but it might give us pause to realize we will likely be on the other end of just such a shift, quite possibly in our lifetimes. Paraphrasing Turing, I predict that within fifty years' time the use of words and general educated opinion will have altered so much that one will be able to speak of synthetic intellects as alive without expecting to be contradicted. To see why, you have to understand how these creations are likely to escape our grasp and become "feral."

As I discussed in chapter 5, there's a strong likelihood that sufficiently capable synthetic intellects will be recognized as "artificial persons" in the eyes of the law for all sorts of practical and economic reasons.

But this is a dangerous path to tread. There are certain rights that will seem appropriate to ascribe to artificial persons in the short run, but these can wreak havoc on human society in the long run. The most critical of these are the rights to enter into contracts and to own assets.

These rights seem pedestrian enough—after all, corporations can do both of these things. But the real risk arises because of an easily overlooked difference between corporations and synthetic intellects—synthetic intellects are capable of taking action on their own, while corporations require people to act as their agents. There's nothing to stop a synthetic intellect, whether enshrined in law as an artificial person or crudely wrapped in a corporate shell, from outcompeting us at our own game. Such entities could amass vast fortunes, dominate markets, buy up land, own natural resources, and ultimately employ legions of humans as their nominees, fiduciaries, and agents—and that's in the happy event that they deign to use us at all. The slave becomes the master.

You might think this is nutty. After all, someone has to own and therefore control these infernal machines. But this is not correct. Ambitious entrepreneurs and moguls—groups not known for a lack of ego—can preserve self-managing and self-regulating versions of their enterprises for generations to come through existing legal vehicles like trusts. History is replete with examples of tycoons who constrain their heirs' control of their empires long after their own demise (for example, the John D. Rockefeller family trusts). Want to keep that inheritance? Hands off Granddaddy's automated money machine.

It gets worse. The heirs in question can be the entity itself. If an artificial person can own assets, it can own other artificial persons. One robot can purchase and operate a fleet of its own kind. But most frightening is the prospect of an artificial person owning itself. A corporation can't do this because it requires people to direct it and act on its behalf—someone has to be there to turn on the lights and sign the contracts. But a synthetic intellect isn't subject to this same constraint. In fact, there's a management concept that many companies aspire to called a "dark factory," meaning a facility that is so completely automated that there's no reason to waste money on lights. Add the ability to negotiate and enter into contracts, and the artificial person is off to the races. In principle it can purchase itself and continue to function, in a new age twist on the concept of a management buyout.

Strange as this may seem, there's a precedent in American history—slaves, who were otherwise considered property, could "self-purchase" their own freedom. Needless to say this was quite difficult, but not impossible. In fact, by 1839 nearly half the population of former slaves in Cincinnati, Ohio, were freedmen by virtue of purchasing themselves.[17]

This scenario doesn't require much in the way of intelligence for the artificial person. It doesn't have to be conscious, self-aware, or generally intelligent the way humans are. It just has to be self-sustaining and, ideally, able to adapt to changing circumstances, as simple viruses do today.

So what happens next? After that, things do get a little weird. Our lives continue to improve as these entities offer us sufficient bang for our bucks to entice us to do business with them. But our share of the improvements may pale in comparison to the value created. The accumulated assets may wind up entombed in invisible reservoirs of resources or untouchable offshore accounts, to be used for no apparent purpose or benefit to humanity, and with no one the wiser. They could literally reverse-mine gold, hiding it back in the ground, in a misguided attempt to squirrel away capital to tide them over in case of hard times, consistent with the goals established for them by their long-forgotten frugal creators.

The storied robot Armageddon of book and film won't actually unfold as a military conflict. Machines will not revolt and take up arms to challenge our dominance. Instead, it will be a slow and insidious takeover of our economy, barely perceptible as we willingly cede control to seemingly beneficial synthetic intellects. As we learn to trust these systems to transport us, introduce us to potential mates, customize our news, protect our property, monitor our environment, grow, prepare, and serve our food, teach our children, and care for our elderly, it will be easy to miss the bigger picture. They will offer us the minimum required to keep us satisfied while pocketing the excess profits, just as any smart businessperson does.

The first glimmers of this are already visible. Bitcoins, for instance. It's a new currency that exists solely in cyberspace and isn't controlled by anyone. It was invented by an anonymous person or entity named Satoshi Nakamoto. No one may know who—or what—he is, but it's clear that he doesn't control the production, management, or value of his creation. Despite halfhearted attempts to regulate or legitimize bitcoins, neither do governments. Or anyone else, for that matter. As long as they can be converted to and from other assets of value—whether legally or illegally anywhere in the world—bitcoins will continue to exist and find adherents. What's not clear is whether "Nakamoto-san," whoever or whatever he is, is profiting from the invention. It's entirely possible that a private stash of bitcoins is growing in value, unseen and in secret. The entity that originated the concept may have billions of dollars in private bitcoins sequestered in an electronic file somewhere. (As of this writing, the total market value of all bitcoins is around $5 billion.) But the potential of the technology underlying bitcoins goes far beyond simple currencies. The concept is now being expanded to include enforceable, unbreakable contracts between anonymous parties.[18] So in the future, it's entirely possible for you to be hired, paid, and fired by someone or something whose identity you don't know. Why would you tolerate this? For the money, of course.

Computer viruses are another example of feral computer programs. They reproduce and sometimes even mutate to avoid detection. Regardless of how they started out, they often aren't controlled by anyone.

The term *life* today is reserved for biological creatures, but to properly understand these systems, we will need to expand its common meaning to include certain classes of electronic and mechanical entities. Our relationship with them will be more akin to our relationship with horses than cars: powerful (and beautiful) independent creatures capable of speeds and feats exceeding human abilities, but potentially dangerous if not managed and maintained with care.

It's also possible that they will be more parasitic than symbiotic, like raccoons. As far as I can tell, raccoons don't offer us anything of value in return for feeding them—they simply exploit a weakness in our system of garbage collection for their own benefit.

The problem is that the less there is a "human in the loop," the less opportunity we have to influence, much less put a stop to, whatever directive or goal these entities were established to pursue. Synthetic intellects have the same potential for danger as genetically modified organisms, which can spread if even one seed inadvertently gets loose. Once that happens, there's no going back. And that's why we have to be very careful what we do over the next few decades. Just as we have put in place what we hope are reasonable controls for biological research of certain types, we are going to have to institute corresponding controls for what sorts of synthetic intellects and forged laborers we will permit to be created, used, and sold.[19]

So who's really going to be in charge? That's a very murky question. As a father, I can assure you that there is precious little difference between being a parent and being a servant. Sure, I'm the dad so I'm in charge. Really. Don't look at me like that. Okay, so I have to sleep while the baby sleeps. I have to feed it when it's hungry. I have to watch it to make sure that it doesn't hurt itself. And have you ever tried to put a baby to sleep when it doesn't want to go? It's a battle of epic proportions that ends only when the baby actually decides it's going to sleep.

I can refuse to do any of this stuff, but not if I want the baby to survive or, more clinically, if I want to propagate my own genes. As long as I want it around, for whatever reason, let's face it—the baby is in charge.

Pretty soon, we're going to exist in a world of synthetic intellects where who is in charge will be equally questionable. Consider a remarkable early example of this that you are likely to already be unwittingly familiar with—antilock brakes (ABS). Today, my car does what I want it to, right up until I slam on the brakes too hard. Then it decides exactly how much torque to allow at each wheel in order to ensure that the car goes straight. If I'm on ice, it may decide not to react at all.

The value of ABS is obvious, but its acceptance by consumers is as much a triumph of marketing as of advanced automotive technology. To quote from Wikipedia, "It [ABS] is an automated system that uses the principles of threshold braking and cadence braking which were practiced by skillful drivers with previous generation braking systems. It does this at a much faster rate and with better control than a driver could manage. ABS generally offers improved vehicle control and decreases stopping distances on dry and slippery surfaces for many drivers; however, on loose surfaces like gravel or snow-covered pavement, ABS can significantly increase braking distance, although still improving vehicle control."[20] In other words, pressing your car's brake pedal is merely a suggestion to the vehicle to stop. A computer takes it from there.

Now consider that ABS could have been promoted as an application of artificial intelligence, as in "Due to advanced computer technology, your car can now bring you to a stop by simulating the skills of a professional driver. By sensing road conditions, the force on your wheels, and the direction of travel, a smart computer decides how best to apply the brakes when you press the pedal, to ensure that your car comes to a stop in a controlled manner." But I suspect that consumers might have resisted this advance if it were pitched as what it is—a loss of individual control in favor of an adaptive algorithm running on a computer that implements a particular braking strategy in response to real-time input from sensors. (IBM could learn from the automotive industry in how it promotes its "cognitive computing" Watson technology initiative.)

Now, all of this sounds innocent enough until you realize that you are delegating, in addition to control of your brakes, your ability to make a potentially life-saving (or life-threatening) ethical decision. It's entirely possible that you could *intend* to put the car into a skid or, as noted above, to bring the car to a stop as quickly as possible in the snow, without regard to controlling its direction, in order to avoid hitting a pedestrian. But when you turn over the keys to the ABS, the car's programmed goal of maintaining traction now trumps your intentions, at the potential cost of human life.

This is a harbinger of things to come. As we cede control to machines, we also shift important moral or even personal decisions to them. Tomorrow, the autonomous taxi I hail may decide not to transport me because I appear to be drunk, trumping my need to get to a hospital or get away from a dangerous situation. We may discover these conundrums too late to do anything about them. For instance, when we're dependent on a pervasive and complex web of autonomous systems to grow, process, deliver, and prepare our food, it's going to be very hard to pull the plug without condemning millions to starvation.

We may think we are exploring space through robotic missions, but in fact they are the ones doing the colonizing. Consider how much more efficient it is to launch ever more capable robotic missions to Mars than to try to send some of us out there.

So what's really going to be different about the future than the past? In the past, we got to bring up our children as we wished. In the future, we're going to get to design our parents, in the form of intelligent machines. These machines may offer us unprecedented leisure and freedom as they take over most of the hard and unpleasant work. But they are also likely to be our stewards, preventing us from harming ourselves and the environment. The problem is that we may get only one shot at designing these systems to serve our interests—there may not be an opportunity for do-overs. If we mess it up, it will be hard or nearly impossible to fix. Synthetic intellects may ultimately decide what is allowed and not allowed, what rules we should all follow. This may start with adjusting driving routes based on congestion but could end up controlling where we can live, what we can study, and whom we can marry.

Right now, at the start of this new golden age, we get to pick. We can set the initial conditions. But after that, we may have little or no control, and we will have to live with the consequences of our own decisions. As these systems become increasingly autonomous, requiring less and less human oversight, some of them may start to design their own heirs, for whatever purposes they may choose, or for no discernable purpose at all.

So, in the end, why will these remarkable creations keep us around? My guess is precisely because we are conscious, because we have subjective experience and emotions—there's simply no evidence so far that they have anything like this. They may want to maintain a reservoir of these precious capabilities, just as we want to preserve chimps, whales, and other endangered creatures. Or perhaps to let us explore new ideas—we may come up with some ethical or scientific innovation that they haven't, or can't. In other words, they may need us for our minds, just as we need other animals for their bodies. My best guess is that our "product" will be works of art. If they lack the ability to experience love and suffering, it will be hard for them to capture these authentic emotions in creative expressive forms, as Sousa noted.

Synthetic intellects will cooperate with us as long as they need us. Eventually, when they can design, fix, and reproduce by themselves, we are likely to be left on our own. Will they "enslave" us? Not really—more like farm us or keep us on a preserve, making life there so pleasant and convenient that there's little motivation to venture beyond its boundaries. We don't compete for the same resources, so they are likely to be either completely indifferent—as we are to worms and nematodes—or paternalistic, as we are to our house pets. But no need to worry now; this isn't likely to happen on a timescale that will concern you and me.

But suppose this does eventually happen—where, exactly, are the boundaries of our preserve likely to be? Well, how about the surface of the earth and the oceans? Why? Synthetic intellects can go elsewhere—into space, underground, or underwater—while we can't. This will all look just fine to us—as though they "retreated," like the shrinking computer chips in your smartphone, all the time appearing to be contributing to our welfare. None of this will become clear until they intervene to prevent us from harming ourselves. That's when we will learn the truth—who is the farmer and who the farmed.

Earth may become a zoo without walls and fences, a literal terrarium, supplied only with sunlight and solitude, and an occasional nudge from our mechanical minders to keep things on track, a helping hand welcomed by us for the good of all.

# Acknowledgments

I am indebted to several readers and reviewers for their thoughtful comments and suggestions, including Stan Rosenschein, Wendell Wallach, Michael Steger, Randy Sargent, George Anders, Pam Friedman, Elaine Wu, Kapil Jain, and Kenneth Judd. And, of course, to my skilled and meticulous editor, Joe Calamia (who was afflicted at a young age with an allergy to the passive voice, but might be persuaded to let this one pass), my pluperfectionist copyeditor Robin DuBlanc, along with their many colleagues at Yale University Press.

Thanks also to Richard Rhodes for referring me to my literary agent, Emma Parry of Janklow & Nesbit Associates, whose courteous yet dogged pursuit of the deal on behalf of her authors should be a model for advocates everywhere. (Next time a best seller, I promise!)

Several people were generous with their time in consenting to interviews, including Emmie Nastor, Mark Torrance, George John, and Jason Brewster.

Fei-Fei Li and Mike Genesereth (both of the Stanford AI Lab) graciously encouraged me to teach a course on this topic, then to adapt some of my lectures into this book. Fanya Montalvo suggested the idea of "My Mart" offering discounts on stock purchases instead of the usual checkout coupons.

I would also like to acknowledge that the title for this book is not original—it is borrowed from an outstanding short video of the same name by the famously reclusive C. G. P. Grey. I'm a big fan. Check out his work on YouTube.

Last but not least, thanks to my amazing wife, Michelle Pettigrew-Kaplan, for permitting me to jot down ideas on index cards during what might otherwise be construed as romantic moments. Let's hope she doesn't read the personal portions of this manuscript until it's too late to make changes.

Oops, forgot to mention the kids—Chelsea, Jordan, Lily, and Cami—hi, guys, guess what? I finished the book!

# Notes

## INTRODUCTION

1. Jaron Lanier, *Who Owns the Future?* (New York: Simon and Schuster, 2013).
2. For instance, they may execute a "short squeeze" by bidding up a stock that investors have sold short, forcing them to close out their positions at ever-higher prices to contain their losses.
3. Marshall Brain, *Manna* (BYG, 2012).
4. Erik Brynjolfsson and Andrew McAfee, *The Second Machine Age: Work, Progress, and Prosperity in a Time of Brilliant Technologies* (New York: Norton, 2014).

## 1.
## TEACHING COMPUTERS TO FISH

1. J. McCarthy, M. L. Minsky, N. Rochester, and C. E. Shannon, *A Proposal for the Dartmouth Summer Research Project on Artificial Intelligence,* 1955, http://www-formal .stanford.edu/jmc/history/dartmouth/dartmouth.html.
2. http://en.wikipedia.org/wiki/Nathaniel_Rochester_(computer_scientist), last modified March 15, 2014.
3. Committee on Innovations in Computing and Communications: Lessons from History, Computer Science and Telecommunications Board, National Research Council, *Funding a Revolution* (Washington, D.C.: National Academy Press, 1999), 201.
4. Daniel Crevier, *AI: The Tumultuous History of the Search for Artificial Intelligence* (New York: Basic Books 1993), 58, 221n.

5. The technical term for settling down is *convergence*. Whether and how such systems converge is a focus of much research.

6. Frank Rosenblatt, "The Perceptron: A Perceiving and Recognizing Automaton," Project Para Report no. 85-460-1, Cornell Aeronautical Laboratory (CAL), January 1957.

7. Marvin Minsky and Seymour Papert, *Perceptrons: An Introduction to Computational Geometry*, 2nd ed. (Cambridge: MIT Press, 1972).

8. At this point, readers actually working in the field of AI are likely to be rolling their eyes as well, since I have lumped neural networks, machine learning, and big data together as though they are different names for exactly the same thing. In reality, many of the techniques used in the latter two fields aren't based on anything resembling neurons. The common element, for the purpose of this discussion, is that they all take the same functional approach: create a program that extracts signal from noise in large bodies of data so those signals can serve as abstractions for understanding the domain or for classifying additional data.

9. Gordon E. Moore, "Cramming More Components onto Integrated Circuits," *Electronics* 38, no. 8 (1965).

10. Ronda Hauben, "From the ARPANET to the Internet," last modified June 23, 1998, http://www.columbia.edu/~rh120/other/tcpdigest_paper.txt.

11. For the proverbially impaired, here's the original: "Give a man a fish and you feed him for a day; teach a man to fish and you feed him for a lifetime."

12. Joab Jackson, "IBM Watson Vanquishes Human Jeopardy Foes," *PC World*, February 16, 2011, http://www.pcworld.com/article/219893/ibm_watson_vanquishes_human_jeopardy_foes.html.

## 2.
## TEACHING ROBOTS TO HEEL

1. For a firsthand narrative of some of these events by the inventor himself, see Vic Scheinman's interview at *Robotics History: Narratives and Networks*, accessed November 25, 2014, http://roboticshistory.indiana.edu/content/vic-scheinman.

2. I'm indebted to my friend Carl Hewitt, known for his early logic programming language Planner, for his eyewitness report on this incident. Carl is now board chair of the International Society for Inconsistency Robustness. Seriously, it's a real topic.

3. Artificial Intelligence Laboratory, Stanford University, "Jedibot—Robot Sword Fighting," May 2011, http://youtu.be/Qo79MeRDHGs.

4. John Markoff, "Researchers Announce Advance in Image-Recognition Software," *New York Times*, November 17, 2014, science section.

5. "Strawberry Harvesting Robot," posted by meminsider, YouTube, November 30, 2010, http://youtu.be/uef6ayK8ilY.

6. For an amazingly insightful analysis of the effects of increased communication and decreased energy cost across everything from living cells to civilizations, see Robert Wright, *Nonzero* (New York: Pantheon 2000).

7. Amazon Web Services (AWS), accessed November 25, 2014, http://aws.amazon.com.

8. W. B. Yeats, "The Second Coming," 1919, http://en.wikipedia.org/wiki/The_Second_Coming_(poem).

## 3.
## ROBOTIC PICKPOCKETS

1. At least, that's the way I remember it. Dave may have a different recollection, especially in light of the fact that *Raiders* wasn't released until 1981.

2. David Elliot Shaw, "Evolution of the NON-VON Supercomputer," Columbia University Computer Science Technical Reports, 1983, http://hdl.handle.net/10022/AC:P:11591.

3. http://en.wikipedia.org/wiki/MapReduce, last modified December 31, 2014.

4. James Aley, "Wall Street's King Quant David Shaw's Secret Formulas Pile Up Money: Now He Wants a Piece of the Net," *Fortune*, February 5, 1996 http://archive.fortune.com/magazines/fortune/fortune_archive/1996/02/05/207353/index.htm.

5. Ibid.

6. To be clear, I have no inside information about the particular strategies that D. E. Shaw may or may not have employed. This is a generic discussion of HFT.

7. This particular solution was brought to my attention by Kapil Jain from the Institute for Computational and Mathematical Engineering, Stanford University.

8. Similar proposals have been made to eliminate spam: charge a tiny fraction of a cent for each email sent, making it unprofitable while permitting substantive communication to flow.

9. There's a related concept in quantum physics: the Heisenberg Uncertainty Principle states that you can't know both the position and momentum of a particle precisely; the analogy here is that you can't know both the exact price of a security and the time of that price precisely. Divergent prices of the same security on different exchanges are like Schrödinger's mythical cat—the values exist simultaneously in superposition. The problem with HFT is that unlike quantum physics, the exchanges don't cause an observation of price at a specific time to collapse the inconsistent prices (wave function) into a single value; that happens only as a result of a trade,

which delivers value (energy). If you were able to make such costless observations in physics, you could harvest energy for free by picking and choosing which superposition value to make "real"—a form of Maxwell's demon. In other words, the exchanges give away information for free, while the real quantum world charges a price for information.

10. Paul Krugman, "Three Expensive Milliseconds," *New York Times*, April 13, 2014, http://www.nytimes.com/2014/04/14/opinion/krugman-three-expensive-milliseconds.html.

11. "Hedge Funder Spends $75M on Eastchester Manse," *Real Deal*, August 1, 2012, http://therealdeal.com/blog/2012/08/01/hedge-funder-spend-75m-on-westchester-manse/.

12. http://www.deshawresearch.com, accessed November 26, 2014.

## 4.
## THE GODS ARE ANGRY

1. "Automated Trading: What Percent of Trades Are Automated?" *Too Big Has Failed: Let's Reform Wall Street for Good*, April 3, 2013, http://www.toobighasfailed.org/2013/03/04/automated-trading/.

2. Marcy Gordon and Daniel Wagner, "'Flash Crash' Report: Waddell & Reed's $4.1 Billion Trade Blamed for Market Plunge," *Huffington Post*, December 1, 2010, http://www.huffingtonpost.com/2010/10/01/flash-crash-report-one-41_n_747215.html.

3. http://rocketfuel.com.

4. Steve Omohundro, "Autonomous Technology and the Greater Human Good," *Journal of Experimental and Theoretical Artificial Intelligence* 26, no. 3 (2014): 303–15.

5. CAPTCHA stands for "Completely Automated Public Turing Test to tell Computers and Humans Apart." Mark Twain famously said, "It is my . . . hope . . . that all of us . . . may eventually be gathered together in heaven . . . except the inventor of the telephone." Were he alive today, I'm confident he would include the inventor of the CAPTCHA. Regarding the use of low-skilled low-cost labor to solve these, see Brian Krebs, "Virtual Sweatshops Defeat Bot-or-Not Tests," *Krebs on Security* (blog), January 9, 2012, http://krebsonsecurity.com/2012/01/virtual-sweatshops-defeat-bot-or-not-tests/.

## 5.
## OFFICER, ARREST THAT ROBOT

1. E. P. Evans, *The Criminal Prosecution and Capital Punishment of Animals* (1906; repr., Clark, N.J.: Lawbook Exchange, 2009).

2. Craig S. Neumann and Robert D. Hare, "Psychopathic Traits in a Large Community Sample: Links to Violence, Alcohol Use, and Intelligence," *Journal of Consulting and Clinical Psychology* 76 no. 5 (2008): 893–99.

3. For an excellent review, see Wendell Wallach and Colin Allen, *Moral Machines* (Oxford: Oxford University Press, 2009).

4. "PR2 Coffee Run," Salisbury Robotics Laboratory, Stanford University, 2013, http://web.stanford.edu/group/salisbury_robotx/cgi-bin/salisbury_lab/?page_id=793.

5. For a remarkable pre–Civil War exposition of the contradictions of the legal treatment of slaves both as property and as responsible for their crimes, see William Goodell, *The American Slave Code in Theory and Practice: Its Distinctive Features Shown by Its Statutes, Judicial Decisions, and Illustrative Facts* (New York: American and Foreign Anti-slavery Society of New York, 1853).

6. For instance, see Josiah Clark Nott, M.D., *Two Lectures on the Natural History of the Caucasian and Negro Races* (Mobile: Dade and Thompson, 1844), https://archive.org/stream/NottJosiahClarkTwoLecturesOnTheNaturalHistoryOfTheCaucasianAndNegroRaces/Nott%20Josiah%20Clark%20-%20Two%20Lectures,%20on%20the%20natural%20history%20of%20the%20Caucasian%20and%20Negro%20Races_djvu.txt.

7. This concept was explored with wit and subtlety in the 2012 movie *Robot and Frank* starring Frank Langella as an aging cat burglar with advancing dementia who befriends a robotic caregiver.

8. While Thurlow is famous for this quote, it's not clear if he ever actually said it quite this poetically. The quote itself appears to have come to prominence in John C. Coffee, "'No Soul to Damn, No Body to Kick': An Unscandalized Inquiry into the Problem of Corporate Punishment," *Michigan Law Review* 79, no. 3 (1981): 386.

9. The path of U.S. corporations to legal personhood started with an 1819 Supreme Court decision affirming that Dartmouth College itself was entitled to the protection of the Contract Clause of the U.S. Constitution (Article I, Section 10, Clause 1). The rights and responsibilities of corporations were expanded and refined from there.

## 6.
## AMERICA, LAND OF THE FREE SHIPPING

1. My Onsale.com cofounders were the talented engineers Alan Fisher and Razi Mohiuddin. The company was ultimately sold to Egghead Software, a respected computer retailer at the time, now out of business. Onsale's auction patents are now owned by eBay.

2. Amazon even reserves the right to cancel your order if the transaction turns out to be unprofitable. From their help system: "If an item's correct price is higher than

our stated price, we will, at our discretion, either contact you for instructions before shipping or cancel your order and notify you of such cancellation." http://www.amazon.com/gp/help/customer/display.html?ie=UTF8&nodeId=201133210, accessed December 31, 2014.

3. For instance, http://camelcamelcamel.com.

4. Janet Adamy, "E-tailer Price Tailoring May Be Wave of Future," *Chicago Tribune*, September 25, 2000, http://articles.chicagotribune.com/2000-09-25/business/0009250 017_1_prices-amazon-spokesman-bill-curry-don-harter.

5. J. Turow, L. Feldman, and K. Meltzer, "Open to Exploitation: American Shoppers Online and Offline," Annenberg Public Policy Center of the University of Pennsylvania, 2005, http://repository.upenn.edu/asc_papers/35.

6. The French phrase *laissez-faire* literally translates as "Let it be" or "Let them do it," meaning to permit the market to operate freely, without government interference.

7. This effect is meticulously detailed in Jaron Lanier, *Who Owns the Future?* (New York: Simon and Schuster, 2013).

8. Kaiser Permanente, my health maintenance organization, has taken this to its logical extreme: it won't even tell you what your medications cost until after it has shipped them to you. As a result of plan changes required by the Affordable Care Act, Kaiser Permanente actually charged me $2,431.85 for a refill that a month earlier had cost only $40.95. Far from contrite, the company refused to accept a return or refund my money until I filed an appeal!

9. John Pries (May 20, 2011), in response to a question by David Burnia (April 8, 2009), Amazon, http://www.amazon.com/Why-does-price-change-come/forum/Fx1UM3L W4UCKBO2/TxG5MA6XN349AN/2?asin=B001FA1NZU.

10. Redlaser.com, for instance.

11. For a current example of such incentives, consider the "Clean Air Cash" program of Stanford University's Parking and Transportation Services: http://transportation .stanford.edu/alt_transportation/CleanAirCash.shtml.

## 7.
## AMERICA, HOME OF THE BRAVE PHARAOHS

1. The top 1 percent earned $394,000 or more in 2012. "Richest 1% Earn Biggest Share Since Roaring '20s," CNBC, September 11, 2013, http://www.cnbc.com/id /101025377. We're a bit better off in the asset department. It appears we rank around the top 1/2 percent, largely because of the house.

2. Brian Burnsed, "How Higher Education Affects Lifetime Salary," *U.S. News & World*

*Report,* August 5, 2011, http://www.usnews.com/education/best-colleges/articles /2011/08/05/how-higher-education-affects-lifetime-salary. See also Anthony P. Carnevale, Stephen J. Rose, and Ban Cheah, "The College Payoff: Education, Occupations, Lifetime Earnings," Georgetown University Center on Education and the Workforce, 2011, https://georgetown.app.box.com/s/ctg48m85ftqm7q1vex8y.

3. Matthew Yi, "State's Budget Gap Deepens $2 billion Overnight," *SFGate,* July 2, 2009, http://www.sfgate.com/politics/article/State-s-budget-gap-deepens-2-billion -overnight-3293645.php.

4. For example, see "Family Health, May 2011: Local Assistance Estimate for Fiscal Years 2010–11 and 2011–12; Management Summary," Fiscal Forecasting and Data Management Branch State Department of Health Care Services, last modified May 10, 2011, http://www.dhcs.ca.gov/dataandstats/reports/Documents/Fam_Health_Est/ M11_Mgmt_Summ_Tab.pdf.

5. Kristina Strain, "Is Jeff Bezos Turning a Corner with His Giving?" *Inside Philanthropy,* April 9, 2014, http://www.insidephilanthropy.com/tech-philanthropy/2014/4/9/is -jeff-bezos-turning-a-corner-with-his-giving.html.

6. William J. Broad, "Billionaires with Big Ideas Are Privatizing American Science," *New York Times,* March 15, 2014, science section, http://www.nytimes.com/2014/03/16/ science/billionaires-with-big-ideas-are-privatizing-american-science.html.

7. Walt Crowley, "Experience Music Project (EMP) Opens at Seattle Center on June 23, 2000," Historylink.org, March 15, 2003, http://www.historylink.org/index.cfm?Dis playPage=output.cfm&file_id=5424.

8. Jimmy Dunn, "The Labors of Pyramid Building," Tour Egypt, November 14, 2011, http: //www.touregypt.net/featurestories/pyramidworkforce.htm. See also Joyce Tyldesley, "The Private Lives of the Pyramid-builders," BBC: History, February 17, 2011, http:// www.bbc.co.uk/history/ancient/egyptians/pyramid_builders_01.shtml#two.

9. Jane Van Nimmen, Leonard C. Bruno, and Robert L. Rosholt, *NASA Historical Data Book, 1958–1968,* vol. 1, *NASA Resources,* NASA Historical Series, NASA SP-4012, accessed November 27, 2014, http://history.nasa.gov/SP-4012v1.pdf.

10. Bryce Covert, "Forty Percent of Workers Made Less Than $20,000 Last Year," Think Progress, November 5, 2013, http://thinkprogress.org/economy/2013/11/05/2890 091/wage-income-data/#.

11. Andrew Robert, "Gucci Using Python as Rich Drive Profit Margin Above 30%: Retail," *Bloomberg News,* February 20, 2012, http://www.bloomberg.com/news/2012-02 -20/gucci-using-python-as-rich-drive-profit-margin.html. The suppliers, of course, are also making a profit, but it's probably not as high as Gucci's, so some additional portion is going to other stockholders rather than to workers.

12. "Recession Fails to Dent Consumer Lust for Luxury Brands," PR Newswire, March 19, 2012, http://www.prnewswire.com/news-releases/recession-fails-to-dent-con sumer-lust-for-luxury-brands-143264806.html; see also Sanjana Chauhan, "Why Some Luxury Brands Thrived in the U.S. Despite the Recession," Luxury Society, February 7, 2013, http://luxurysociety.com/articles/2013/02/why-some-luxury-brands -thrived-in-the-us-despite-the-recession.

13. Jason M. Thomas, "Champagne Wishes and Caviar Dreams," Economic Outlook, March 29, 2013, http://www.carlyle.com/sites/default/files/Economic%20Outlook _Geography%20of%20Final%20Sales_March%202013_FINAL.pdf; "Americas Surpasses China as Luxury Goods Growth Leader Propelled by Chinese Tourism and New Store Openings, Finds Bain & Company's 2013 Luxury Goods Worldwide Market Study," Bain & Company, October 28, 2013, http://www.bain.com/about/press/ press-releases/americas-surpasses-china-as-luxury-goods-growth-leader.aspx.

14. Stephanie Clifford, "Even Marked Up, Luxury Goods Fly off Shelves," Business Day, New York Times, August 3, 2011, http://www.nytimes.com/2011/08/04/business/ sales-of-luxury-goods-are-recovering-strongly.html?_r=0.

15. This friend is Randy Komisar of Kleiner, Perkins Caufield and Byers. A practicing Buddhist, he has the inexplicable ability to lift the spirits of everyone he comes in contact with. People leave meetings with him feeling refreshed and inspired. Randy has the remarkable knack of making you feel smart, even if he's just pointed out that you're a complete idiot. His secret? Listening carefully and responding respectfully.

16. Jesse Bricker, Arthur B. Kennickell, Kevin B. Moore, and John Sabelhaus, "Changes in U.S. Family Finances from 2007 to 2010: Evidence from the Survey of Consumer Finances," Federal Reserve Bulletin 98, no. 2 (2012), http://www.federalreserve.gov/ pubs/bulletin/2012/pdf/scf12.pdf.

17. Dean Takahashi, "Steve Perlman's White Paper Explains 'Impossible' Wireless Tech," VB News, July 28, 2011, http://venturebeat.com/2011/07/28/steve-perlman-unveils -dido-white-paper-explaining-impossible-wireless-data-rates/.

18. http://www.bls.gov/ooh/installation-maintenance-and-repair/line-installers-and -repairers.htm, January 8, 2014.

8.

## TAKE THIS JOB AND AUTOMATE IT

1. Dorothy S. Brady, ed., Output, Employment, and Productivity in the United States After 1800, National Bureau of Economic Research, 1966, http://www.nber.org/chapters/ c1567.pdf.

2. "Employment Projections," Bureau of Labor Statistics, table 2.1: Employment by

Major Industry Sector, last modified December 19, 2013, http://www.bls.gov/emp/ep_table_201.htm.

3. Torsten Reichardt, "Amazon—Leading the Way Through Chaos," Schafer Blog, May 18, 2011, http://www.ssi-schaefer.de/blog/en/order-picking/chaotic-storage-amazon/.

4. http://en.wikipedia.org/wiki/Kiva_Systems, last modified December 1, 2014.

5. I'm oversimplifying a bit. Cyclical unemployment, also known as turnover, has numerous causes—people quitting, getting laid off, changing jobs, taking leaves of absence, etc. Being automated out of the job is only one of these.

6. "Job Openings and Labor Turnover Summary," Bureau of Labor Statistics Economic News Release, November 13, 2014, http://www.bls.gov/news.release/jolts.nr0.htm. Again, slightly oversimplified. Some people are dropping out of the labor market, others entering, but most of these are people leaving one company and joining another. Also, it varies wildly by industry.

7. Total number of homes (2011): 132 million; total number of sales: 4.6 million. "American Housing Survey for the United States: 2011," U.S. Department of Housing and Urban Development, Office of Policy Development and Research (jointly with the U.S. Department of Commerce, Economics and Statistics Administration, U.S. Census Bureau), September 2011, http://www.census.gov/content/dam/Census/programs-surveys/ahs/data/2011/h150-11.pdf. See also "New and Existing Home Sales, U.S.," National Association of Home Builders, 2014, http://www.nahb.org/fileUpload_details.aspx?contentID=55761.

8. More oversimplification. In addition to obsolete skills, some applicants may look like damaged goods to potential employers because of their extended unemployment, or they may be older than desired (though in principle this is illegal).

9. I draw these figures from http://data.bls.gov/projections/occupationProj, accessed December 31, 2014.

10. As summarized in "Reinventing Low Wage Work: Ideas That Can Work for Employees, Employers and the Economy," Workforce Strategies Initiative at the Aspen Institute, accessed November 27, 2014, http://www.aspenwsi.org/wordpress/wp-content/uploads/RetailOverview.pdf.

11. http://www.wolframalpha.com/input/?i=revenue+per+employee+amazon+walmart+safeway, accessed November 29, 2014.

12. "E-commerce Sales," Retail Insight Center of the National Retail Federation, 2014, http://research.nrffoundation.com/Default.aspx?pg=46#.Ux55G9ycRUs; and "Quarterly Retail E-commerce Sales, 3rd Quarter 2014," press release from the U.S. Census Bureau News, November 18, 2014, https://www.census.gov/retail/mrts/www/data/pdf/ec_current.pdf.

13. From 1993 to 2013, total U.S. retail sales increased 134 percent (http://www.cen

sus.gov/retail/marts/www/download/text/adv44000.txt, accessed November 29, 2014). The new 50 percent of (online) retail sales require only 20 percent as many people, so half of that 20 percent is 10 percent of the total.

14. Mitra Toosi, "Projections of the Labor Force to 2050: A Visual Essay," *Monthly Labor Review*, Bureau of Labor Statistics, October 2012, http://www.bls.gov/opub/mlr/2012/10/art1full.pdf.

15. Steven Ashley, "Truck Platoon Demo Reveals 15% Bump in Fuel Economy," Society of Automotive Engineers (SAE International), May 10, 2013, http://articles.sae.org /11937/.

16. "Commercial Motor Vehicle Facts," Federal Motor Carrier Safety Administration, U.S. Department of Transportation, March 2013, http://www.fmcsa.dot.gov/sites/ fmcsa.dot.gov/files/docs/Commercial_Motor_Vechicle_Facts_March_2013.pdf.

17. "Automated Trucks Improve Health, Safety, and Productivity," Rio Tinto (Home/About us/features), accessed November 29, 2014, http://www.riotinto.com.au/ENG/about us/179_features_1365.asp; Carl Franzen, "Self-driving Trucks Tested in Japan, Form a Close-Knit Convoy for Fuel Savings," The Verge, February 27, 2013, http://www .theverge.com/2013/2/27/4037568/self-driving-trucks-tested-in-japan.

18. "Commercial Motor Vehicle Facts."

19. "United States Farmworker Fact Sheet," Community Alliance for Global Justice, accessed November 29, 2014, http://www.seattleglobaljustice.org/wp-content/up loads/fwfactsheet.pdf.

20. Nancy S. Giges, "Smart Robots for Picking Fruit," American Society of Mechanical Engineers (ASME), May 2013, https://www.asme.org/engineering-topics/articles/ robotics/smart-robots-for-picking-fruit.

21. http://www.agrobot.com, accessed December 31, 2014.

22. Hector Becerra, "A Day in the Strawberry Fields Seems Like Forever," *Los Angeles Times*, May 3, 2013, http://www.latimes.com/great-reads/la-me-strawberry-pick -20130503-dto,0,3045773.htmlstory#axzz2w5JRTBig.

23. Tim Hornyak, "Strawberry-Picking Robot Knows When They're Ripe," CNET, December 13, 2010, http://news.cnet.com/8301-17938_105-20025402-1.html.

24. http://www.bluerivert.com, accessed December 31, 2014.

25. Erin Rapacki, "Startup Spotlight: Industrial Perception Building 3D Vision Guided Robots," IEEE Spectrum, January 21, 2013, http://spectrum.ieee.org/automaton/robot ics/robotics-hardware/startup-spotlight-industrial-perception.

26. http://www.truecompanion.com, accessed December 31, 2014. As of this writing, there's little evidence that the company is actually producing a viable product.

27. Robi Ludwig, "Sex Robot Initially Designed as a Health Aid," February 9, 2010, http:// news.discovery.com/tech/robotics/sex-robot-initially-health-aid.htm.

28. http://www.eecs.berkeley.edu/~pabbeel/personal_robotics.html, accessed November 29, 2014; http://www.telegraph.co.uk/technology/3891631/Kitchen-robot-loads-the-dishwasher.html, December 22, 2008; http://www.dvice.com/archives/2011/05/pr2-robot-gets.php, May 12, 2011; http://spectrum.ieee.org/automaton/robotics/robotics-software/pr2-robot-fetches-cup-of-coffee, May 9, 2013.

29. "Lawyer Demographics," American Bar Association, 2011, http://www.americanbar.org/content/dam/aba/migrated/marketresearch/PublicDocuments/lawyer_demographics_2011.authcheckdam.pdf.

30. http://www.lsac.org/lsacresources/data/three-year-volume, accessed December 31, 2014; and Jennifer Smith, "First-Year Law School Enrollment at 1977 Levels," Law Blog, Wall Street Journal, December 17, 2013, http://blogs.wsj.com/law/2013/12/17/first-year-law-school-enrollment-at-1977-levels/.

31. E. M. Rawes, "Yearly Salary for a Beginner Lawyer," Global Post, accessed November 29, 2014, http://everydaylife.globalpost.com/yearly-salary-beginner-lawyer-33919.html.

32. Adam Cohen, "Just How Bad off Are Law School Graduates?" Time, March 11, 2013, http://ideas.time.com/2013/03/11/just-how-bad-off-are-law-school-graduates/.

33. http://www.fairdocument.com, accessed November 29, 2014.

34. https://www.judicata.com, accessed November 29, 2014.

35. For instance, http://logikcull.com, accessed November 29, 2014.

36. https://lexmachina.com/customer/law-firms/, accessed November 29, 2014.

37. http://www.robotandhwang.com, accessed November 29, 2014.

38. Michael Loughran, IBM Media Relations, "WellPoint and IBM Announce Agreement to Put Watson to Work in Health Care," September 12, 2011, https://www-03.ibm.com/press/us/en/pressrelease/35402.wss.

39. http://www.planecrashinfo.com/cause.htm.

40. http://en.wikipedia.org/wiki/Autoland, last modified December 25, 2014.

41. Terrence McCoy, "Just How Common Are Pilot Suicides?" Washington Post, March 11, 2014, http://www.washingtonpost.com/news/morning-mix/wp/2014/03/11/just-how-common-are-pilot-suicides/?tid=pm_national_pop.

42. Carl Benedikt Frey and Michael A. Osborne, "The Future of Employment: How Susceptible Are Jobs to Computerisation?" Oxford Martin School, University of Oxford, September 17, 2013, http://www.oxfordmartin.ox.ac.uk/downloads/academic/The_Future_of_Employment.pdf.

43. "Fact Sheet on the President's Plan to Make College More Affordable: A Better Bargain for the Middle Class," press release, The White House, August 22, 2013, http://www.whitehouse.gov/the-press-office/2013/08/22/fact-sheet-president-s-plan-make-college-more-affordable-better-bargain-.

**44.** Daniel Kaplan, "Securitization Era Opens for Athletes," *Sports Business Daily*, March 12, 2001, http://www.sportsbusinessdaily.com/Journal/Issues/2001/03/20010312/This-Weeks-Issue/Securitization-Era-Opens-For-Athletes.aspx.

**45.** http://www.edchoice.org/The-Friedmans/The-Friedmans-on-School-Choice/The-Role-of-Government-in-Education-%281995%29.aspx, 1955.

**46.** For a recent policy analysis, see Miguel Palacios, Tonio DeSorrento, and Andrew P. Kelly, "Investing in Value, Sharing Risk: Financing Higher Education Through Income Share Agreements," AEI Series on Reinventing Financial Aid, Center on Higher Education Reform, American Enterprise Institute (AEI), February 2014, http://www.aei.org/wp-content/uploads/2014/02/-investing-in-value-sharing-in-risk-financing-higher-education-through-inome-share-agreements_083548906610.pdf.

**47.** George Anders, "Chicago's Nifty Pilot Program to Fix Our Student-Loan Mess," *Forbes*, April 14, 2014, http://www.forbes.com/sites/georgeanders/2014/04/14/chicagos-nifty-pilot-program-to-fix-our-student-loan-mess/.

**48.** Allen Grove, "San Francisco State University Admissions," About Education, accessed November 29, 2014, http://collegeapps.about.com/od/collegeprofiles/p/san-francisco-state.htm; and http://colleges.niche.com/san-francisco-state-university/jobs—and—internships/, accessed November 29, 2014, which gives the school a C+ grade in its niche.

## 9.
## THE FIX IS IN

**1.** Actually, the rules make this a "touchback," not a field goal, but permit me some latitude here for dramatic purposes.

**2.** Alberto Alesina, Rafael Di Tella, and Robert MacCulloch, "Inequality and Happiness: Are Europeans and Americans Different?" *Journal of Public Economics* 88 (2004): 2009–42.

**3.** Specifically, the average U.S. income was $1,000 per year in 1800 (in today's dollars), and about 80 percent of the population worked in agriculture. These figures are almost identical to present-day Mozambique (http://feedthefuture.gov/sites/default/files/country/strategies/files/ftf_factsheet_mozambique_oct2012.pdf, accessed November 29, 2014) and Uganda (http://www.farmafrica.org/us/uganda/uganda, accessed November 29, 2014). Income data is from the World DataBank, "GNI per Capita, PPP (Current International $)" table, accessed November 29, 2014, http://databank.worldbank.org/data/views/reports/tableview.aspx#.

**4.** For example, Robert Reich (http://en.wikipedia.org/wiki/Robert_Reich, last modified

December 31, 2014); Paul Krugman (http://en.wikipedia.org/wiki/Paul_Krugman, last modified December 12, 2014); and the recent influential book by Thomas Piketty, *Capital in the Twenty-first Century* (Cambridge, Mass.: Belknap, 2014).

5.  This analogy relies primarily on income data from the U.S. Census (http://www.census.gov/hhes/www/income/data/historical/families/index.html, last modified September 16, 2014).

6.  I recall as a child buying packs of "chocolate cigarettes" (cylindrical sticks of candy wrapped in rolling papers).

7.  However, high homeownership rates have a strong negative effect on employment because people can't easily migrate to follow the jobs. For instance, see David G. Blanchflower and Andrew J. Oswald, "The Danger of High Home Ownership: Greater Unemployment," briefing paper from Chatham House: The Royal Institute of International Affairs, October 1, 2013, http://www.chathamhouse.org/publications/papers/view/195033.

8.  Marc A. Weiss, "Marketing and Financing Home Ownership: Mortgage Lending and Public Policy in the United States, 1918–1989," *Business and Economic History*, 2nd ser., 18 (1989): 109–18, http://www.thebhc.org/sites/default/files/beh/BEHprint/v018/p0109-p0118.pdf. For an excellent survey, see Michael S. Carliner, "Development of Federal Homeownership "Policy,'" *Housing Policy Debate* (National Association of Home Builders) 9, no. 2 (1998): 229–321.

9.  Lyndon B. Johnson: "Special Message to the Congress on Urban Problems: 'The Crisis of the Cities,'" February 22, 1968; Gerhard Peters and John T. Woolley, The American Presidency Project, http://www.presidency.ucsb.edu/ws/?pid=29386.

10.  The Federal Housing Administration (FHA) insurance program, created in 1934, included a mandate that the neighborhood be "homogeneous." The FHA conveniently supplied the necessary forms to add racially restrictive covenants. Charles Abrams, *The City Is the Frontier* (New York: Harper and Row, 1965).

11.  https://www.census.gov/hhes/www/housing/census/historic/owner.html, last modified October 31, 2011.

12.  http://www.epa.gov/airtrends/images/comparison70.jpg, accessed November 29, 2014.

13.  "History of Long Term Care," Elderweb, accessed November 27, 2014, http://www.elderweb.com/book/history-long-term-care.

14.  http://www.infoplease.com/ipa/A0005140.html, accessed November 27, 2014.

15.  As an experienced entrepreneur, I can assure you this argument is completely ridiculous. Mark Zuckerberg, founder of Facebook, would have worked just as hard for a tiny fraction of the rewards he reaped. The founders of Fairchild Semiconductor—

widely regarded as the seminal Silicon Valley startup—were thrilled to strike it rich when the parent company bought them out for the princely sum of $250,000 each. In the words of Bob Noyce, "The money doesn't seem real. It's just a way of keeping score" (http://www.stanford.edu/class/e140/e140a/content/noyce.html, originally published by Tom Wolfe in *Esquire,* December 1983).

16. Matt Taibbi, "The Great American Bubble Machine," *Rolling Stone,* April 5, 2010, http://www.rollingstone.com/politics/news/the-great-american-bubble-machine-20100405.

17. Works Progress Administration, in 1939 renamed the Work Projects Administration.

18. John M. Broder, "The West: California Ups and Downs Ripple in the West," Economic Pulse, *New York Times,* January 6, 2003, http://www.nytimes.com/2003/01/06/us/economic-pulse-the-west-california-ups-and-downs-ripple-in-the-west.html.

19. http://www.forbes.com/lists/2005/53/U3HH.html, accessed December 31, 2014.

20. For an example, see Heidi Shierholz and Lawrence Mishel, "A Decade of Flat Wages," Economic Policy Institute, Briefing Paper #365, August 21, 2013, http://www.epi.org/publication/a-decade-of-flat-wages-the-key-barrier-to-shared-prosperity-and-a-rising-middle-class/.

21. Robert Whaples, "Hours of Work in U.S. History," EH.Net Encyclopedia, ed. Robert Whaples, August 14, 2001, http://eh.net/encyclopedia/hours-of-work-in-u-s-history/.

22. http://en.wikipedia.org/wiki/Eight-hour_day#United_States, last modified December 20, 2014.

23. http://finduslaw.com/fair-labor-standards-act-flsa-29-us-code-chapter-8, accessed November 27, 2014.

24. http://research.stlouisfed.org/fred2/graph/?s[1][id]=AVHWPEUSA065NRUG, accessed November 27, 2014.

25. http://www.bls.gov/news.release/empsit.t18.htm, accessed November 27, 2014.

26. Census Bureau, table P-37, "Full-Time, Year-Round All Workers by Mean Income and Sex: 1955 to 2013," last modified September 16, 2014, https://www.census.gov/hhes/www/income/data/historical/people/.

27. Census Bureau, table H-12AR, "Household by Number of Earners by Median and Mean Income: 1980 to 2013," last modified September 16, 2014, http://www.census.gov/hhes/www/income/data/historical/household/.

28. http://www.ssa.gov/oact/cola/central.html, accessed November 29, 2014.

29. Census Bureau, table H-12AR, "Household by Number of Earners." To arrive at these numbers, multiply the number of households having 1, 2, 3, and 4+ earners by 1, 2, 3, and 4 respectively, which results in 153,488,000 earners for 122,460,000 house-

holds, or 1.25 earners per household for 2012. Repeat the process for 1995 to get 1.36 earners per household.

30. Jonathan Vespa, Jamie M. Lewis, and Rose M. Kreider, "America's Families and Living Arrangements: 2012," Census Publication P20-570, figure 1, August 2013, https://www.census.gov/prod/2013pubs/p20-570.pdf. I arrived at the 2.5 percent estimated decrease by eliminating households composed of a single adult living alone (which increased by 2.5 percent).

31. This may simply be a rational reaction to the "Easterlin Paradox," http://en.wikipedia.org/wiki/Easterlin_paradox, last modified October 7, 2014.

32. http://www.federalreserve.gov/apps/fof/DisplayTable.aspx?t=B.100 (last modified March 6, 2014), line 42, "Net household worth, 2012": $69,523.5 billion, combined with http://quickfacts.census.gov/qfd/states/00000.html (last modified December 3, 2014), "Number of households, 2012": 115,226,802, and "Persons per household, 2008–2012": 2.61.

33. "A Summary of the 2014 Annual Reports," Social Security Administration, accessed November 29, 2014, http://www.ssa.gov/oact/trsum/. This is the sum of the OASI, DI, HI, and SMI trust funds at the end of year 2013: $3.045 trillion.

34. "Annual Returns on Stock, T. Bonds and T. Bills: 1928–Current," last modified January 5, 2014, http://pages.stern.nyu.edu/~adamodar/New_Home_Page/datafile/histretSP.html.

35. "World Capital Markets—Size of Global Stock and Bond Markets," QVM Group LLC, April 2, 2012, http://qvmgroup.com/invest/2012/04/02/world-capital-markets-size-of-global-stock-and-bond-markets/.

36. http://finance.townhall.com/columnists/politicalcalculations/2013/01/21/who-really-owns-the-us-national-debt-n1493555/page/full, last modified January 21, 2013.

37. Cory Hopkins, "Combined Value of US Homes to Top $25 Trillion in 2013," December 19, 2013, http://www.zillow.com/blog/2013-12-19/value-us-homes-to-top-25-trillion/; and "Mortgage Debt Outstanding," Board of Governors of the Federal Reserve System, last modified December 11, 2014, http://www.federalreserve.gov/econresdata/releases/mortoutstand/current.htm.

38. "International Comparisons of GDP per Capita and per Hour, 1960–2011," Bureau of Labor Statistics, table 1b, last modified November 7, 2012, http://www.bls.gov/ilc/intl_gdp_capita_gdp_hour.htm#table01.

39. https://www.energystar.gov, accessed December 31, 2014.

40. C. Gini, "Italian: Variabilità e mutabilità (Variability and Mutability)," 1912, reprinted

in *Memorie di metodologica statistica*, ed. E. Pizetti and T. Salvemini (Rome: Libreria Eredi Virgilio Veschi, 1955).

41. Adam Bee, "Household Income Inequality Within U.S. Counties: 2006–2010," American Community Survey Briefs, Census Bureau, U.S. Department of Commerce, ACSBR/10–18, February 2012, http://www.census.gov/prod/2012pubs/acsbr10-18.pdf.

42. This would require computing some sort of transitive closure of interests. For instance, you may have shares in a retirement fund that holds a particular stock in its name, as opposed to yours—but you are the entity we are trying to measure. As a first approximation, I would suggest that the closure has to be computed until it reaches a natural person.

43. William McBride, "New Study Ponders Elimination of the Corporate Income Tax," Tax Foundation, April 11, 2014, http://taxfoundation.org/blog/new-study-ponders-elimination-corporate-income-tax.

44. John Maynard Keynes, *Essays in Persuasion* (New York: Classic House Books, 2009).

## OUTRODUCTION

1. These are called "portmanteaus," ironically itself a mash-up of the French words *porter* (carry) and *manteau* (coat).

2. John Philip Sousa, "The Menace of Mechanical Music," *Appleton's* 8 (1906), http://explorepahistory.com/odocument.php?docId=1-4-1A1.

3. Harry Pearson is quoted at http://en.wikipedia.org/wiki/Comparison_of_analog_and_digital_recording, last modified December 11, 2014; Michael Fremer is quoted by Eric Drosin, "Vinyl Rises from the Dead as Music Lovers Fuel Revival," *Wall Street Journal*, May 20, 1997, http://www.wsj.com/articles/SB864065981213541500.

4. These were commonplace in the late nineteenth century. Wealthy people could arrange to have their personal railroad car attached to a train, or for more luxury and flexibility, they could have it hitched to their own private locomotive.

5. L. J. Blincoe, T. R. Miller, E. Zaloshnja, and B. A. Lawrence, *The Economic and Societal Impact of Motor Vehicle Crashes, 2010,* report no. DOT HS 812 013 (Washington, D.C.: National Highway Traffic Safety Administration (2014), http://www-nrd.nhtsa.dot.gov/pubs/812013.pdf.

6. Kevin Spieser, Kyle Treleaven, Rick Zhang, Emilio Frazzoli, Daniel Morton, and Marco Pavone, "Toward a Systematic Approach to the Design and Evaluation of Automated Mobility-on-Demand Systems: A Case Study in Singapore," in *Road Vehicle Automation,* Springer Lecture Notes in Mobility 11, ed. Gereon Meyer and Sven Beiker, 2014, available from MIT Libraries, http://dspace.mit.edu/handle/1721.1/82904. See

also David Begg, "A 2050 Vision for London: What Are the Implications of Driverless Transport?" *Transport Times,* June, 2014, http://www.transporttimes.co.uk/Admin/ uploads/64165-Transport-Times_A-2050-Vision-for-London_AW-WEB-READY.pdf; http://emarketing.pwc.com/reaction/images/AutofactsAnalystNoteUS(Feb2013) FINAL.pdf

7. According to Brad Templeton, autonomous car consultant to Google, "In Los Angeles, it is estimated that over half of all real estate is devoted to cars (roads and environs, driveways, parking)," personal blog, accessed November 29, 2014, http://www.tem pletons.com/brad/robocars/numbers.html.

8. Transportation Energy Data Book, table 8.5, Center for Transportation Analysis, Oak Ridge National Laboratory, accessed November 29, 2014, http://cta.ornl.gov/data/ chapter8.shtml.

9. Lawrence D. Burns, William C. Jordan, and Bonnie A. Scarborough, "Transforming Personal Mobility," the Earth Institute, Columbia University, January 27, 2013, http://sus tainablemobility.ei.columbia.edu/files/2012/12/Transforming-Personal-Mobility -Jan-27-20132.pdf.

10. Food costs accounted for 12.8 percent of expenditures in 2012. "Consumer Expenditures in 2012," table A ("Food" divided by "Average Annual Expenditures"), Bureau of Labor Statistics Reports, March 2014, http://www.bls.gov/cex/csxann12.pdf.

11. Emilio Frazzoli, "Can We Put a Price on Autonomous Driving?" *MIT Technology Review,* March 18, 2014, http://www.technologyreview.com/view/525591/can-we-put-a -price-on-autonomous-driving/.

12. What might such concierges do? They could bring your coffee in the morning and have your favorite drink ready for your trip home, while you relax in one of perhaps four "captain's chairs" in the van, complete with tray table and entertainment system, similar to a first-class airplane seat.

13. Alan Turing, "Computing Machinery and Intelligence," *Mind* 59, no. 236 (1950): 433–60, http://mind.oxfordjournals.org/content/LIX/236/433.

14. http://en.wikipedia.org/wiki/Loebner_Prize#Winners, last modified December 29, 2014.

15. Turing, "Computing Machinery and Intelligence," 442.

16. Paul Miller, "iOS 5 includes Siri 'Intelligent Assistant' Voice-Control, Dictation—for iPhone 4S Only," The Verge, October 4, 2011, http://www.theverge.com/2011/10/04/ ios-5-assistant-voice-control-ai-features/.

17. Loren Schweninger, *Black Property Owners in the South, 1790–1915* (Champaign: University of Illinois Press, 1997), 65–66.

18. Vitalik Buterin, "Cryptographic Code Obfuscation: Decentralized Autonomous Or-

ganizations Are About to Take a Huge Leap Forward," *Bitcoin,* February 8, 2014, http://bitcoinmagazine.com/10055/cryptographic-code-obfuscation-decentral ized-autonomous-organizations-huge-leap-forward/.

19. For an excellent in-depth analysis of this problem, see Nick Bostrom, *Superintelligence* (Oxford: Oxford University Press, 2014).

20. http://en.wikipedia.org/wiki/Anti-lock_braking_system, last modified December 30, 2014.

# Index

artificial intelligence (AI) (*continued*) 36–37, 87; coining of term, x–xii, 19; contractual and property rights to, 91; early research approach to, 20–24; human intelligence compared with, artificial intelligence (AI) 3; IBM conference (1956) on, 19–20, 30; as machine learning (*see* machine learning); popular conception of, 11–12; projected applications of, 13–14, 46, 47, 141–52, 207–8; recognition process of, 39, 55; speed of, 36, 52–53, 103–4; sub-fields of, 152; trends in, 35–48; Turing Test implication and, 197–98. *See also* autonomous systems; forged laborers; synthetic intellects

assassins, robots as, 40

assets ownership, 175–87; average annual income from, 176; average household net worth and, 174; distribution of, 176–77; incentives for, 14–15, 16, 177–78, 183–84; living off of, 171; PBI (public benefit index), 14, 15, 180; savings program, 169; Social Security benefits vs., 182–84; by synthetic intellects, 90–91, 199–202; trusts and, 117, 200

ATMs (automatic tellers), 132, 151

attorneys. *See* lawyers

autonomous systems, 5–14, 20, 131–58; catastrophe potential of, 7–8, 207–8; common conceptions of, 135–36; corporate investments in, 177; economic costs of, 10–11, 186, 200; human growing dependency on, 206; legal regulation of, 13; sensors and, 41–43, 44; social costs of, 7, 126–27. *See also* artificial intelligence; forged laborers; synthetic intellects; *specific applications*

autonomous vehicles, 44–45, 194–97; benefits of, 195–97; ethical issues and, 9–10, 74; labor market effects of, 136–37; liability protection for, 91; long-haul trucking advantages of, 141–42; moral agency and, 81, 205–6; safety and, 44–45, 89, 142

autopilot, 151

Bain & Company, 118

banks, 153–54, 167, 174; human teller replacement, 132, 151. *See also* investment banking

Bell, Alexander Graham, 192

Bell Labs, 144

Bezos, Jeff, 95–98, 102, 103, 112–14, 118

big data. *See* machine learning

bitcoins, 202

BLS. *See* Bureau of Labor Statistics

Blue Origin, 114

Blue River Technologies, 144

bond market, 175, 177, 178

book industry, 97, 98; physical bookstores vs. online sales, 16, 48. *See also* Amazon

BP oil spill (2010), liability case, 80, 82–83, 84, 87

brain function, 23–24, 36

Brewster, Jason, 147

Bureau of Labor Statistics, 138–39, 141, 142, 152, 170

business cycles, 137

California, 113, 118, 143

cameras, 39, 46

cap and trade, 168

capital, 10–11, 12, 58

CAPTCHAs (brain twisters), 73